LET'S-TALK-ABOUT-IT STORIES FOR KIDS

You Are Wonderfully Made!

LOIS WALFRID JOHNSON

Illustration by Virginia Peck

NAVPRESS ●®
A MINISTRY OF THE NAVIGATORS
P.O. BOX 6000, COLORADO SPRINGS, COLORADO 80934

The Navigators is an international Christian organization. Jesus Christ gave His followers the Great Commission to go and make disciples (Matthew 28:19). The aim of The Navigators is to help fulfill that commission by multiplying laborers for Christ in every nation.

NavPress is the publishing ministry of The Navigators. NavPress publications are tools to help Christians grow. Although publications alone cannot make disciples or change lives, they can help believers learn biblical discipleship, and apply what they learn to their lives and ministries.

Second printing, 1989

Printed in the United States of America

CONTENTS

To every boy and girl
who has the courage
to dream big
and follow in the footsteps
of Jesus Christ.

AUTHOR

When Lois Walfrid Johnson was nine years old she wondered, "What do I want to be when I grow up?" She sensed God's call to be a writer. If she could possibly write a book, she wanted to tell others what she believed about Jesus Christ.

That desire stayed with her through high school, college, and the early years of her marriage to Roy Johnson, an elementary school teacher. When the youngest of their three children entered first grade, Lois became a full-time free-lance writer. Her articles, poetry, and books have been published in English-speaking countries throughout the world and translated into nine languages.

Lois Johnson is the author of thirteen books,

including *Secrets of the Best Choice*, *You're Worth More Than You Think!*, and *Thanks For Being My Friend* in the *LET'S TALK ABOUT IT* series. She has also written *Just a Minute, Lord* and *You're My Best Friend, Lord* for pre-teens; *Come as You Are* for young teens; *Gift in My Arms, Either Way, I Win*, and *Falling Apart or Coming Together* for adults. Lois leads seminars and retreats and speaks at churches and conferences throughout the United States.

ACKNOWLEDGMENTS

My warm thanks to each of the following: Diane Brask, Betty Coleman, Maude Dahlberg, Leland Evenson, Jerry Foley, Peggy Hackett, Cynthia Johnson, Charette Kvernstoen, Elaine Roub, Penny Stokes, James Walfrid, Terry White, and the Grantsburg, Wisconsin, Public Library for help with the manuscript; all those who have faithfully prayed about the writing of this book and the others in the series; my husband, Roy, for his ideas, his love for children, and his daily caring for me, both professionally and personally.

As a writer, I value the person who changes the way I work by offering encouragement, insight, and gracious honesty. While editing this series, Traci Mullins has been that gift to me.

A NOTE TO PARENTS

It has often been said that Christian values are better caught than taught. Perhaps this is most true in the area of sexuality. Day by day children sense your attitudes, your respect for the way God created you, your belief in the sacredness of sex within marriage.

But concepts about sexuality should also be discussed. Your child needs correct information on which to build godly attitudes. Your willingness to talk in a natural way will communicate even more—that you value who you are as a sexual being, and that your child's sexuality is normal and wonderful.

You Are Wonderfully Made! was written to help you in those conversations. It goes beyond information about human development to deal with attitudes and values from a Christian viewpoint. It presents situations that may be encountered by children in this age group or slightly older.

With the other titles in this series, you probably read the stories together, as you came to them. Because of the wide variation in children's maturity levels, you may want to read this book before giving it to your son or daughter. Then plan a time for talking together and discussing questions. Or read the stories together, explaining concepts in your own words. Take the stories in sequence, over a period of time. Or turn directly to a topic that relates to something happening that day.

Up to now, your child may have had questions he or she has not asked. Reading these stories will encourage the freedom to do so. If you're not comfortable with some questions, be honest about your feelings. But then, be willing to seek out answers. Your son or daughter will feel it's all right to ask real questions.

God bless you in the adventure of talking about values important to you and your child.

TO KIDS WHO READ THIS BOOK

This book is about miracles.

"Miracles?" you may ask.

Yep, that's right. Miracles about you.

"But miracles are something so big, so unusual that. . . ."

That you never hope to be in on one?

"Right," you say. "Isn't God the One in charge of miracles?"

Yep, right again. God's the One in charge. But there's something you might need to think about. Miracles are all around you every minute of the day. Yet you may not see them. Or if you see them, you don't think of them as miracles.

Take that honey sitting on your breakfast table.

This morning you put some on your toast and didn't give it a second thought. But did you know that to make one pound of honey, bees may travel 13,000 miles? That's crossing the United States from New York to California four times!

Then there's the only bird that can fly backward or hover like a helicopter in one spot. You guessed it—the hummingbird! When they've just hatched, ruby-throated babies are so small that a teaspoon holds four of them. Yet within three weeks they're fully feathered and strong enough to leave the nest.

And what about those tulips growing outside your house? In the winter they seem dead and maybe covered by snow. But every spring little green shoots push their way through the earth. Soon a bud appears, then a full-blown flower. What makes that tulip keep trying year after year? Why does it push its way up to grow into something beautiful for you?

There are other, even bigger miracles. Each time you look in the mirror, you see one. Maybe you're saying, "I don't even like the way I look. I sure don't feel like a miracle!" That's okay. You don't have to *feel* like one. Just the same, you *are*.

Do you know your heart pumps five quarts of blood through your body in about sixty seconds? In one year your heart pumps from 777,000 to over 1,600,000 gallons—enough to fill 97 to 200 railroad tank cars of 8,000 gallons each! When you think about that, do you suppose that maybe, just possibly, you're one of God's miracles?

This book will tell you about the miracle of how you came to be. It will help you understand the miracle of sex and why you're created the way you are. But this book also talks about more—your sexuality.

Sexuality has to do with how your being a boy or girl affects your entire life. How do you feel about yourself because you're male or female? What attitudes do you have? How does the way you think about your sex affect your relationships?

Your sexuality involves your feelings, your mind, and your spirit, as well as your body. It involves your beliefs and your values. That's where choices come in.

Because your body is changing, you'll have new choices to face. That's part of growing up. Making those choices can be fun, but also difficult, because you're choosing what side you want to be on. The side you're on will make a difference in the kind of person you become.

"But . . ." you say, "I don't *know* what side I want to be on."

The kids in this book often feel the same way. Like you, they need to choose God's side. But there's another side wanting to win. That's the side of sex you often see in movies and videos or on TV. That's the side you learn about from kids at school who don't love God. That's the side you hear from people who don't know that God created sex to be something beautiful. That same God created you in His own image—to be like Him.

As you read this book, you may find that the information in a certain story doesn't seem important to you right now. If so, that's okay. Go on to the next chapter. Later, when you face questions about that topic, go back to the story you missed.

The more difficult words will be in italics like *this*. If you want help in pronouncing those words or understanding their meaning, check the list at the back of the book.

At the end of each story you'll find questions. Or you may have ones of your own. Talk about them with your mom or dad or another grownup you trust. Think of ways to solve the problems the kids in the stories face. Think of ways to solve your own problems. Then turn the book upside down. Repeat the Bible verse to yourself until you receive the help it gives. Read the prayer or pray one of your own.

When you think about all that's changing in your life, it may seem a bit scary to you. You may wonder, "What if I make a wrong choice? Or a lot of wrong choices? What if I'm a loser?" Or, "What if kids make fun of me?"

Sometimes it helps to know what the Bible says about Jesus when He was twelve years old: "Jesus grew both in body and in wisdom, gaining favor with

God and men" (Luke 2:52, GNB). Whatever you face, you can think about Jesus. You can ask yourself, "What would He do?" Then you can ask Him to help you do it.

The God of miracles, who created you and made you the person you are, has given you another miracle—His Son Jesus.

So, are you ready? Then let's begin. Remember, *you are wonderfully made!*

MITZI LOOKS IN THE MIRROR

As the water from the shower sprayed on Mitzi's back, she felt good all over. It was Saturday morning, and the day stretched out before her. "No homework!" she thought. As soon as she finished dusting a couple of rooms, she could do whatever she wanted.

Coming out of the shower, Mitzi caught a glimpse of herself in the mirror. For a moment she stood there, looking at her body. "I'm changing," she thought. Mitzi liked what she saw and wondered how it would feel to be a woman.

She was still wondering as she dusted Mom's bedroom. There she discovered a new book. Dropping down on the floor, Mitzi started turning the pages.

"This is *exactly* what I want to know!"

Just then Mom came in. "Oh, good, you found the book. I bought it for you yesterday. Why don't you read it, and then we can talk, okay?"

Mitzi went to her room and started right in. The first chapter was about how every living thing grows:

A helpless kitten becomes a cat able to hunt her own food. A slender-legged fawn loses its spots and begins to look like its mother. A one-inch baby kangaroo, or joey, changes into a powerful traveler.

Human beings also grow. You changed from an infant into a toddler. You learned to talk and run and climb. You started to attend school. There you learned to study and use your mind. As you played with other children, you developed physically and emotionally.

You discovered what it means to become responsible—to do those things your parents ask you to do. As they learned they could trust you, they began giving you more freedom. They let you try new things.

During all those changes, your *pituitary gland* regulated most of your growth. Located at the base of your brain, the pituitary is the master gland of your body.

When your body reaches the age of *puberty*, there's another change. The word puberty describes the time when a boy or girl becomes physically mature enough to reproduce life. That doesn't mean they're emotionally ready. It takes many more years for that.

At puberty your pituitary gland sends a message to your *ovaries*, two almond-shaped organs in your reproductive system, saying, "Begin sending *hormones!*" These hormones start the development of sexual changes in your body. A boy begins noticing male traits. A girl begins noticing female traits.

For you, as a girl, these changes usually start at about ten or eleven years of age, although they may be a year earlier or a couple of years later. Your breasts start to change their shape, and over a period of years, develop like those of a woman. You notice hair under your arms and in your *pubic* area. The hair on your legs may begin to change, and your hips start to round out.

All of this is normal. They're signs that something else is happening in your body.

Mitzi stopped for a minute to look at the illustrations. Then she continued reading.

In the lower part of your *abdomen* (you probably call it stomach), you have reproductive organs that were very small when you were born. Your two ovaries contain thousands of tiny *eggs*. These are female sex cells. These eggs are so small that you can't see them. But starting at puberty one of them is released about every twenty-eight days. That release of an egg is called *ovulation*.

On the side of each ovary, but not attached to them,

are *Fallopian tubes*. These tubes are hollow inside. On the other end they're attached to the *uterus*, or as the Bible calls it, the *womb*.

When an egg leaves the ovary, it goes through the Fallopian tube. If a male sex cell, or *sperm*, meets the egg in the tube, the egg is *fertilized*. After about four days, the fertilized egg moves down and attaches itself to the wall of the uterus. The egg grows and becomes a baby.

The uterus is shaped like a pear. Because the uterus is hollow inside and made of a stretchy muscle, it expands to give a baby room to grow.

At the bottom of the uterus is a small opening called the *cervix*. This cervix leads to a passageway called the *vagina*. When a baby is born, it passes down through this vagina.

The opening of the vagina lies between a girl's legs and is protected by two soft folds of skin. A girl also has two other openings—the *anus* for passing solid waste and the *urethra*, through which urine passes. The *clitoris* is a small sensitive organ located just above the urethra.

Mitzi stretched. There were still more things she wondered about. But just then Mom came by the door. "How're you doing?" she asked.

"Pretty good," answered Mitzi. "But there're a lot of big words."

Mom dropped down in a chair. "Let's go through that section together. Then I can help you."

As Mom and Mitzi talked, they matched the following words to the correct definitions:

1. ___ puberty
2. ___ ovaries
3. ___ Fallopian tubes
4. ___ vagina
5. ___ pituitary
6. ___ egg
7. ___ ovulation
8. ___ abdomen
9. ___ uterus, or womb
10. ___ hormone
11. ___ sperm

a. pear-shaped organ that holds a growing baby
b. female organs that have thousands of tiny eggs
c. the time when an egg is released from the ovary, occurs about every twenty-eight days
d. the time when a boy or girl is physically able to reproduce life
e. female sex cell
f. stomach
g. passageways through which the egg travels on its way to the uterus
h. passageway a baby passes through to be born
i. master gland of the body
j. male sex cell
k. starts the development of sexual traits in the body of a boy or girl

(Answers on page 185)

TO TALK ABOUT

▶What questions would you like to ask your mom or dad or another adult you trust? They'll want to help you with anything you don't understand.

Know that the LORD is God. It is he who made us, and we are his; we are his people, the sheep of his pasture. (Psalm 100:3)

You're really something, God! It's hard to believe how many things work together in order for me to become a woman. Thanks for the fun of being a girl and being You!

ROB AND DAD TALK

At first the flames of the campfire leapt high in the air. Then, as the logs burned down to embers, Rob and the other boys began making s'mores.

As he put a roasted marshmallow and part of a chocolate bar between graham crackers, Rob grinned. "Want some more, Dad?"

Dad grinned back and reached out for the treat. Leaning against a log, he looked relaxed and happy. Rob felt the same way.

That weekend they'd gone on a father and son camp out. Since Mom and Dad's divorce, Rob didn't see Dad as often and felt glad for the time with him. That morning they'd canoed on the river. After lunch they swam in a quiet inlet near their campground. For both of them it'd been a good day.

Before long, the dads and sons scattered to their own tents. The night air had started to cool down, and Rob crawled into his sleeping bag. Lying there, he decided this might be the time to ask the things he'd wondered about.

"Dad . . ." Rob's voice sounded uncertain.

With the light of a flashlight, Dad was closing the tent flap. "Yep? What can I do for you?"

"Why do some kids my age have hair under their arms and others don't?"

"There's a lot of difference between boys," said Dad. "As far as when they reach *puberty*, I mean."

"What's that?" asked Rob.

"Puberty? It's the time when a boy is physically able to become a father or a girl is able to become a mother. Girls usually reach that stage earlier than boys. A boy will probably enter puberty somewhere between twelve and fifteen years old, but it can be earlier or later."

Dad zipped open the window, and a dim light shone into the tent. Then he sat down on his sleeping bag. "Did you notice today how tall Tony's grown? And he's already got lots of hair on his face. But Jack's the same age and a head shorter. He doesn't have *any* hair on his face."

Dad clicked off the flashlight and crawled into the

sleeping bag next to Rob. "And maybe you noticed something else when everyone showered after swimming. Some boys have hair around their sexual organs and others don't."

Rob had noticed all right, and was afraid to say anything. "You know, I don't understand . . ." Rob stopped, feeling embarrassed. "I don't understand how everything works."

But Dad didn't sound embarrassed. "Do you mean how a boy's reproductive system works? It's really a miracle the way God created you."

For a moment Dad was quiet, as though thinking about where to begin. "It'd be easier if I had a drawing to show you. But you know that behind your penis and between your legs you have a small bag of skin. That's called the *scrotum.*

"Inside the scrotum you have two *testicles.* The testicles have a couple of jobs. They produce *hormones*, which cause a boy to develop hair on his body at puberty—like the hair you noticed. Hormones also make a boy's voice get lower."

"Like Mike's did today? One minute it was high, then it was low. It kind of cracked."

"And he was embarrassed, wasn't he? But he didn't need to be. All of us fathers have been at the same place."

Dad went on, "The testicles also produce *sperm* or male sex cells. Sperm are very small—smaller than the sharp end of a fish hook."

"What do they look like?"

"Under a microscope sperm cells look kind of like tadpoles. Remember how we saw tadpoles swimming in shallow water in early spring? How they have little tails? Those little tails help the sperm travel where they need to go.

"There's something else that's really interesting about the way you're created," Dad went on. "In order to survive, sperm need a temperature lower than your normal body temperature. So God put your testicles outside your body in the scrotum. Good idea, huh?"

In the dim light, Rob nodded.

"When a boy reaches puberty, his body also makes a milky liquid. Sperm cells travel up a tiny tube and mix with that liquid. The sperm and liquid together are called *semen*. Then the semen goes out of the body through a small tube in the penis called the *urethra*."

"But that's where I go to the bathroom . . ." Rob stopped.

"You're right," said Dad. "Urine also leaves the body through that same tube in the penis. But urine and semen don't pass from the body at the same time."

A breeze had come up, and Dad closed the flap on the tent window. "There's something else you might wonder about," he said. "Even babies and little boys sometimes have an *erection*. That means their penis becomes firm and stands out from their body. As a boy matures, he begins having more erections.

"He may also have what's called a *wet dream* or nocturnal emission. Sometimes as a boy dreams about girls, his penis becomes erect and semen is released. If you wake up and wonder what's happened, your body is just getting rid of excess semen. It's a normal part of growing up. If your clothes are wet, get up and change them, then go back to sleep.

"Speaking of sleep . . ." Dad reached out and gave Rob's shoulder an affectionate shake. "But we had a good talk, didn't we? If you ever have any more questions. . . ."

"Yep, I'll ask," said Rob, pulling his sleeping bag up around his shoulders. It really had been a good day.

TO TALK ABOUT

▶Rob felt good after he talked with his dad. Do you have more questions? Why don't you talk to your mom or dad or another adult you trust? They'll be glad you asked.

▶ **Match the following:**

1. ___ puberty
2. ___ scrotum
3. ___ ___ functions
    of testicles
4. ___ semen
5. ___ urethra
6. ___ wet dream
7. ___ sperm
8. ___ erection

(Answers on page 185)

a. tube that carries urine and semen
b. male sex cells
c. combination of sperm and milky liquid
d. release of excess semen
e. produces sperm
f. small bag of skin that holds testicles
g. produces hormones
h. when a boy's penis becomes firm and stands out from his body
i. the time when a boy or girl becomes physically able to become a parent

---

God saw all that he had made, and it was very good.
(Genesis 1:31)

Thank You, God, for the way You made me. All the little things You thought of are great! Help me to always respect what it means to be a boy created by You.

SATURDAY WITH MOM

When Mitzi and Mom finished talking about how a girl's body is made, Mitzi felt good about becoming a woman. Later on, she went back to the book Mom had given her. She'd heard girls talk about having a period and wanted to know more. Once again, she started reading:

You've already learned that about every twenty-eight days the ovary releases an egg cell. That egg passes down the Fallopian tube to the uterus.

The uterus, or womb, has a special lining prepared to nourish a baby. It contains many blood vessels that help a baby grow. If no egg has been fertilized, that lining, or tissue, isn't needed. It separates from the uterus. The

31

tissue, along with the egg and waste blood, passes out through the vagina. ·

This process occurs about every twenty-eight days and is called *menstruation.* When girls menstruate they often say, "I'm having my period."

Girls usually have their first period somewhere between the age of nine and fourteen. Normally a period lasts from three to five days. At first the periods may be irregular, with a girl skipping a month or two now and then. As time goes on, her cycle will probably become more regular. By marking a calendar, a girl can know about when her period will take place.

When Mitzi finished reading, she had some questions. She was glad when Mom stopped in her room again. "How will I feel when I have a period?" Mitzi asked.

"Sometimes girls have a little discomfort in their abdomen, or they ache in their lower back. Usually this isn't serious. If you ever have a problem, just tell me. But most girls keep on doing whatever they normally do."

"What do I do if I get my period?"

Mom went to the linen closet and brought back a box. "You can keep these *sanitary napkins* in a drawer so you have them if you start your period."

Mom opened the box. "The napkins will protect your clothes and absorb the blood you pass. When you have your period, it's important to take a shower or bath or wash the *genital* area every day. It's also good to change napkins fairly often—maybe three or four times a day."

"After you've had your periods awhile, you may want to use *tampons* instead of a sanitary pad. A tampon is a small roll of absorbent material you insert into your vagina. You need to change it several times a day to avoid an illness called Toxic Shock Syndrome."

"What if I start having a period when I'm in school?" asked Mitzi.

"Talk to a female teacher or go to the nurse's office. She'll help you," said Mom. "Once you've started having periods you can carry napkins in your purse that time of the month."

"But they took the doors off the toilets."

Mom sighed. "I saw that the last time I was in your school. Why don't you ask the nurse if there's some place with more privacy? Or try asking your gym teacher."

"What if kids know I have my period?"

"They won't," said Mom. "You may feel like they do, but they won't unless you tell them. If you want, you can talk about it to Anna, or another special girlfriend. Maybe Anna will start having periods about the same time. Do you know what'd be fun to do?"

"What?" asked Mitzi.

"When you have your first period, why don't you

and I do something special? We'll celebrate this stage of your becoming a woman. Let's go out to eat or do something like that."

Mitzi grinned. "Okay by me." For a moment she thought about all that would be happening to her body.

"Mommm . . ." Mitzi stopped.

Mom smiled. "Another question? What is it?"

"Sometimes I look forward to growing up, and sometimes I don't."

Mom leaned forward to hug Mitzi. "I know. And it's okay to feel that way. But that's something else God has done for you. When He created your body, He made it so you'll mature at your own pace.

"That may be different from when Anna or one of your other friends matures. Every girl is a little different. One girl will be first to start menstruating or wearing a bra. Another girl will be the last. Those changes will come when your body is ready. Okay?"

Mitzi nodded.

"Any more questions?"

Mitzi grinned. "Not right now. But maybe tomorrow."

TO TALK ABOUT

▶What happens in a girl's body in order for her to have a period?

▶What's the best way to keep track of when your period will be?

▶Some kids talk about sex with just anybody. Why might they pick up wrong information that way?

▶Kids are ready to learn about menstruation or other details about sex at different ages. Your mom or dad may have talked with you when you were eight or nine years old. But other kids may not be ready to understand at that time. Why is it important that you let these kids talk with their parents first?

▶What questions do you have that you'd like to ask your mom or dad or another special person you trust?

And my God will meet all your needs according to his glorious riches in Christ Jesus. (Philippians 4:19)

Thank You, God, for all the special things You did to make me the way I am. Help me when I get upset because my body changes faster or slower than the other girls. Thanks that I don't have to worry about that. Thanks for being the One in charge!

MORE THAN ONE MIRACLE

It was two o'clock in the morning when Joel felt Mom's hand on his shoulder. Through the fog of sleep he heard her voice.

"Taffy's having her puppies. Still want to see them being born?"

Rubbing the sleep out of his eyes, Joel struggled out of bed and headed for the stairs. He'd been waiting for this.

His family had two Labradors—a black male named Fudge and a buff-colored female called Taffy. Now Taffy lay on a blanket in one corner of the large kitchen. As she turned her head, her large brown eyes looked at Joel.

Dad had set up a large piece of cardboard, blocking off that corner of the kitchen. "Taffy knows you. She's so gentle I don't think she'll mind if you watch. But stay back of this so you don't upset her."

One puppy had already been born. As Joel watched, Taffy licked the little body. With its eyes still closed, it was small and helpless.

"Can it see?" asked Joel.

"Nope," said Dad. "A puppy's blind when it's born. It'll open its eyes in about ten days or so."

A few minutes later a second puppy was born. It had a soft clear bag around it. As Joel watched, Taffy broke the bag and freed the puppy from it. Then Taffy licked the little body, washing it off.

By now the first puppy had snuggled up to Taffy's stomach and started drinking milk. Joel pulled up a chair and watched every move. One by one, four more puppies were born. Each one seemed like a miracle.

At last Joel crawled back into bed, but the next day he had some questions. While Mom was fixing supper, Joel found Dad in the living room. "How come Taffy's puppies are different colors?" he asked. "I thought they'd all look like Taffy."

"That's because Fudge is their father," said Dad. "Because he's a black Lab, there're some black and some chocolate puppies. Only one was buff, wasn't it? Because Fudge has dark hair, it shows up in his puppies."

"What do you mean?"

"Lots of times with animals we don't know who the father is. In our case we know it's Fudge. Because he's our dog, he stays here. But usually animals don't have a family the way human beings do."

"Like ours?"

"Yep," said Dad. "Like ours. Babies need both a mother and a father to take care of them. That's why it's important that a mom and dad are committed to each other. Do you know what I mean by commitment?"

Joel thought for a moment. "That you love each other?"

"Right. Love is important. But commitment also means we've promised to help each other. We've promised to be loyal to each other, to stick by each other, even when it's hard. Sometimes a mom or dad dies. Or they're separated by divorce. Those times are very hard for a family. Yet even though a mom and dad are separated by divorce, they still love their children.

"Because God wanted children born within marriage, He made us in such a way that it takes both a mom and a dad to have a baby. Do you understand how a baby is created?"

"Not all of it," said Joel.

"Okay, you know how a boy's body is different from a girl's body. One of God's miracles is that those differences are just what's needed in order to create a baby. The Bible says that when a man and a woman are married they become one flesh.

"A husband and wife like to have special alone times. That's a way of showing their love for each other. Because they're married and committed to each other, those times are very beautiful.

"During those alone times, they may have what we call *sexual intercourse*. A man's penis becomes firm and fits into a woman's vagina. Sperm cells are released from the man's body. Those sperm travel up the uterus into a woman's Fallopian tubes. If an egg has been released from one of the woman's ovaries, the egg and sperm meet.

"Only one sperm cell unites with an egg cell. When that happens, the egg has been fertilized. We say that *conception* has taken place. God has started a new life.

"The fertilized egg cell begins to multiply. One cell becomes two, two become four, until there are more and more cells. The egg moves down and attaches itself to the wall of the uterus. If everything goes well, the cells keep multiplying. Slowly the new baby develops."

"Last night, what was the little bag around Taffy's puppies when they were born?" asked Joel.

"For a human baby it's called an *amniotic sac*, or bag of waters. The amniotic sac is a bag full of liquid that protects the baby from bumps and keeps it the right temperature. The *placenta* is an organ attached to the uterus, and it's full of blood vessels. Food and oxygen, from the mother, flow through those blood vessels and through the *umbilical cord* to the baby."

"The what?"

"The umbilical cord. You know you have a navel? You call it a belly button. Your cord stretched from there to the placenta. That's how you received food and oxygen before you were born. And your waste materials passed through the cord to the placenta."

"How long does it take?"

"For a baby to develop? For human babies about nine months. Your mom's abdomen kept getting bigger until you were ready to be born. I remember how much fun it was to know you were growing."

"So do I!" said Mom, as she came into the room. "By the time you were about thirteen weeks old, your body was completely formed. Yet you were only about three and a half inches long."

Joel grinned.

"One day when the doctor was checking your mom, he brought me in to hear your heartbeat! Then as you got bigger, I often put my hand on your mom's abdomen and felt you kick."

Joel laughed.

"You kept growing until you were ready to be born," said Dad. "When that time comes, the muscles in a woman's uterus begin to squeeze and push the baby down into the vagina. The bag of waters breaks, and the vagina stretches to let the baby pass through."

Dad grinned. "The most special moment of all was when I watched your birth. The minute you were born, the doctor said, 'He's a boy!' You let out a big cry, and I thought, 'Wow! Thank You, God! He sounds healthy!'"

"You got to see me being born?"

"Yep," said Dad. "I was there the whole time. And now some fathers even get to cut the umbilical cord."

"Doesn't that hurt the baby?"

"Nope. It's like cutting hair or fingernails."

"They wrapped you in a blanket and put you in my arms," said Mom. "All I could say was, 'You're beautiful!' I loved you so much that I started to cry."

Inside, Joel felt warmed and loved. Then suddenly he thought of his friend Matt. "What about kids who're adopted?"

"The birth process is just the same," said Dad. "It's just that for one reason or another the mother isn't able to take care of the baby. She allows a mom and dad who want a baby very much to become parents. Are you thinking of Matt?"

Joel nodded.

"The first time his mom and dad saw him was just as exciting for them as when we first saw you. And they love Matt the way we love you."

"Any more questions?" asked Mom.

"Nope!" said Joel. Jumping up, he went out into the kitchen. Taffy's puppies were snuggled up against her, and Joel sat down to watch.

TO TALK ABOUT

▶This story talked about two different miracles for Joel. What were they?

▶Have you ever seen a puppy or kitten being born? Or, if you live on a farm or a ranch, have you seen calves or lambs or other animals being born? What do you remember about those special times?

▶Animals love and protect their new babies. How does your family protect and care for you?

▶How did God plan creation so that children are born in families?

▶What does the word *conception* mean?

▶In what ways does God's miracle of birth seem especially wonderful to you?

For this reason a man will leave his father and mother and be united to his wife, and they will become one flesh. (Genesis 2:24)

I'm beginning to see how great You are, God! Thanks that in order to be born, I needed both a mom and a dad. Thanks for making me one of Your BIG miracles!

I WONDER...

Later on, Mitzi, Rob, and Joel had more questions. Here's what they discovered.

WHAT ABOUT TWINS?

Twins develop in one of two ways. Sometimes a fertilized egg divides completely in two, and two babies develop. In that case, *identical twins* are born. They will be the same sex and look alike.

Other times two sperm cells fertilize two eggs. Then *fraternal twins* are born. They can be the same sex, or one might be a boy and the other a girl. They may be as different as two children in the same family, even though they're born at the same time.

45

WHY AM I A GIRL? OR A BOY?

It has to do with a little thread-like particle called a *chromosome*. When conception takes place, an egg has twenty-three chromosomes and the sperm has twenty-three. There are two kinds of sperm. One is called an X chromosome sperm. When that unites with an egg, a girl is born. The other is called a Y chromosome sperm. When that unites with an egg, a boy is born.

WHAT IS MASTURBATION?

Masturbation is the handling of one's own sexual organs for pleasure. In past years many stories and myths led people to believe that masturbation is physically harmful. Medical authorities now feel that's not true—that masturbation is often a common experience in growing up.

However, masturbation can become a habit that controls a person emotionally and spiritually. Think of a puppy on a long leash tied to a tree in the middle of a yard. If that puppy keeps running around the tree, always in the same direction, he soon finds himself tied close to the tree. He isn't free to run and play with children who come into the yard.

Boys or girls who masturbate can begin to feel like that puppy. They may not be as free to develop in their friendships. Like that puppy, these boys and girls need someone to help them walk the opposite way around the tree.

If you don't feel comfortable talking or praying with someone about this, talk to Jesus. Ask Him to help you so you aren't controlled by this habit. If you've had impure thoughts or daydreams, ask forgiveness, and *know* that Jesus loves you and has forgiven you. Let Him help you leave feelings of guilt behind.

Then go on to other things. Get involved in sports, hobbies, and activities that help you develop friends and good relationships.

WHAT DOES IT MEAN WHEN THE BIBLE TALKS ABOUT CIRCUMCISION?

A boy is born with a loose fold of skin over the end of his penis. *Circumcision* is a simple operation that removes the skin and makes it easier to keep the penis clean.

In Bible times, God told Abraham and his descendants to circumcise their male children. It was a sign that God and His people had a special relationship. The Bible tells us that after Jesus was born, Mary and Joseph took Him to the Temple to be circumcised when He was eight days old.

At the present time, some boys are circumcised

and others aren't. If parents want their son circumcised, a doctor takes care of it soon after the baby's birth.

WHAT IS ACNE?

The word *acne* refers to pimples and blackheads, a problem you may call "zits." Having acne isn't much fun, but it's a common experience for both boys and girls in the years between puberty and adulthood.

Avoid picking or squeezing pimples. They may become infected and leave scars. Because your skin will probably be more oily than it used to be, cleanse it carefully. If you continue to have a problem, ask your mom or dad whether you need to see a skin doctor.

SHORTY'S DISCOVERY

When the phone jangled, Brad was the one who picked it up.

"Hey, Shorty. . . ."

There it was again. Brad felt like not answering.

But the voice on the other end kept talking. "We've got a tournament going at the park today. The Bears against the Tigers, and one of the guys on our team got sick. . . ."

"Aw, Stretch," interrupted Brad without thinking why he called his friend that. "You know I don't like playing volleyball."

"But hey, come on—help us out. The Bears are in a jam."

Brad and Stretch had been friends for years, but

Brad kept thinking up excuses. Stretch wouldn't listen, and Brad was afraid to say what was really wrong.

"How can I tell him I'm too short?" he thought. "I can't get the ball over the net. I can't spike 'em like he does. I'm just a loser."

Stretch acted like he hadn't heard any of Brad's excuses. "I'll stop for you on the way to the park." Before Brad could answer, Stretch hung up.

Half an hour later Stretch pounded on the door. Brad still didn't feel good about playing. This last year Stretch had shot up, and he was now more than a head taller than Brad. To make matters worse, Brad was shorter than everyone his age. For some time he'd been getting out of every volleyball game he could.

"Be great to play with you again, Shorty," said Stretch on the way to the park.

Brad stopped in his tracks, his anger boiling up and spilling over. "I can't *stand* being called Shorty."

"Well, do you think I like being called Stretch?"

"That's different."

"No, it's not. Everywhere I go people turn around and stare at me."

"You mean it's as awful being too tall as too short?"

"You betcha."

"But it'd be great to be tall. You're better in sports. You beat out the other kids."

Stretch laughed, and Brad felt uncomfortable. "Wish I hadn't opened my mouth," he thought.

But when Stretch spoke, his voice was quiet. "I just don't fight it anymore."

"Fight it?"

"The way I am. I can't help that I'm tall, the same way you can't help that you're short. Why fight it?"

"Whadda you mean?"

"It's in the *genes*. My mom and dad are tall, and I'm tall. Your mom and dad are short, and you're short. It's like getting blue eyes or brown hair. So what's the big deal?"

Brad didn't have an answer for that one. From science class he knew that within the *chromosomes* he'd received from his mom and dad were genes. Those genes decided how he'd look—the color of eyes and hair and skin, the shape of his hands and feet, and yes, his height.

Brad thought back to his family's reunion a month before. At least a hundred times he'd heard someone say, "You sure look like your dad!" Brad got tired of hearing about it, yet he had to admit he was glad he did look like Dad—except for being short, that is.

Soon Brad and Stretch reached the park, and Stretch started lining up the Bears. "You stand next to me, Shorty."

"So you can hit all the ones I miss?" Brad wanted to say.

51

But while the Tigers were finding their places, Stretch leaned over and spoke in a soft voice. "Go for the fast ones. Set 'em up, and I'll spike 'em."

"Big deal," thought Brad. "Way to make yourself look good."

When the first ball came his way, Brad tried to spike it himself. It headed straight for the center of the net.

Stretch didn't say anything, and the next chance he got, Brad tried it again. Once more the ball headed into the net and dropped to the ground. The Tiger score jumped ahead: 7 to 9, their favor.

This time Brad caught Stretch looking at him. Brad felt uncomfortable. "I've lost two points for us. Maybe he's right. But why should I help Stretch look good?"

On the next serve, the ball dropped on the other side of Stretch. He started for it, but didn't move fast enough. The ball touched ground, and the Tigers scored again.

"He should've made it," thought Brad. "If I'd been that close, I'd have had it."

In that instant a thought ripped through his mind. "There *is* something I can do better—I can move faster."

There was something different about knowing that. In a quiet moment between the action, Brad thought about it. "That's the way things are." For the first time he wasn't trying to beat out Stretch.

Brad straightened his shoulders and stood ready. "Okay, you old Tigers," he said under his breath. "Get out of our way."

The next time the Bears had the serve, Brad and Stretch were close to the net. When the Tigers volleyed the ball back to them, Brad set it up. Stretch spiked it. Sure enough, the Bears scored!

Before long, Brad knew he and Stretch had a good thing going. When a quick fast move was needed, Brad went for it. More than once he set up the ball. But when they needed a leap or spike, Brad got out of the way, and Stretch took it. The game ended with the Bears winning 15 to 13.

Stretch slapped Brad on the back. "We're a good team, Shorty!"

For once Brad didn't mind his other name.

TO TALK ABOUT

▶ Stretch had learned something important about how to handle his height. What was it?

▶ Kids take growth spurts at different times, and often boys get their height later than girls. But Brad might always be shorter than most other boys. Why? How do genes affect someone's height?

▶ There are many other ways that genes affect the way you look and grow. What are some of them? You might like to check an encyclopedia. Try looking under genes, genetics, and heredity.

▶What did Brad discover about Stretch's playing ability? What ability did Brad offer the team?

▶What was Brad's miracle?

▶What are some things you can't change about yourself? What does it mean to inherit certain traits? What have you inherited?

▶What are ways you can learn new skills or put your inherited abilities to good use?

When my bones were being formed, carefully put together in my mother's womb, when I was growing there in secret, you knew that I was there—you saw me before I was born. (Psalm 139:15-16, GNB)

Thank You, God, for the genes You gave me. Help me to be happy with the things about me I can't change. Help me to develop the inherited abilities You've given me.

NEW HOPE FOR HEIDI

Heidi took the stairs two at a time and headed straight for her bedroom. Slamming the door behind her, she threw herself down on the bed.

Tears pressed against her eyes as she relived that awful moment at school. Two boys had bumped into her—purposely, it seemed.

They'd exclaimed, "Oh, excu-u-u-se me!" Then they'd called her that awful name. Not even to herself would Heidi repeat it. It hurt too much.

Biting her lip, Heidi had kept the tears back, thinking, "Not for anything am I gonna let those creeps know how I feel!"

But now she wondered, "Why, God? Why did I

55

have to develop earlier than the other girls?" For a long time she'd been wearing baggy sweaters. It didn't work anymore. "How can I hide the way I look?"

Just then there came a knock on the bedroom door. "Heidiiii!"

Jumping up, Heidi opened the door. Her seventeen-year-old sister, Cher, popped in. "Wanna go get Mom's birthday present? Dad said I could take the car."

Heidi liked going places with Cher. Somehow she always managed to make things fun. Fifteen minutes later they walked into the mall.

After looking in two stores, Cher said, "Let's try that little place where we went last time. Remember where it is? Can't think of its name."

As they headed into the large open area at the center of the mall, Heidi suddenly stopped. "Let's go somewhere else instead."

"How come?"

"See those boys? They're from school."

Heidi started off in another direction, and Cher followed. "How come you want to ditch 'em?"

Heidi kept walking.

"How come?"

Still Heidi didn't answer. But again she felt like crying, just remembering what happened.

"Hey, come on, I'm your big sis. You can tell me. Let's duck in here, and I'll treat you to a soda."

And so the story came out. Cher listened without talking until Heidi finished. Then she said, "It's just *hormones.*"

"It's what?"

"Hormones. They cause sexual traits to develop—male traits in boys and female traits in girls. That's why your hips are changing too—pretty soon my jeans will fit you."

"But no one else . . ." Heidi broke off. "I mean. . . ."

Cher's voice was soft. "It's not up to you when your hormones kick in. You can't control it. But that's why one girl matures faster than another. And that's okay. For one girl, it'll be early. For another, it'll be late. Either way, it's just normal."

"But I feel so dumb."

"One way isn't right and the other way wrong. It's only what kids make it—especially boys who aren't very smart."

"But it's so awful when they tease me."

"You're right, it is. When I was your age they called me the very same thing."

"They did? What did you do?"

"I cried. I hunched my shoulders, hoping kids wouldn't see. I kept making excuses to not go to school. Finally Mom caught on to what was wrong. She told me all that stuff about my body being a gift from God. I didn't believe her. In fact, I got so mad at one boy I gave him a bloody nose."

Heidi started to giggle, thinking about the boys from school, wondering how they'd feel. "That's what I should do."

"Only it didn't help," said Cher. "The next day the guy brought back his buddies. *All* of them started calling me names. And managed to stay far enough away. . . ."

"So you couldn't slug 'em." Again Heidi giggled.

Cher grinned.

"Then what happened?"

"It took awhile, but finally I got smart. I decided, 'They're having all that fun bugging me. I'm not gonna give 'em the satisfaction.' I considered the source and didn't let 'em get to me."

"But how'd you do that?"

Now Cher's eyes were serious. "Kids who're unhappy on the inside want to make others unhappy. If they can't get through to you, they'll go on to someone else. It's no fun teasing someone who doesn't cry or get mad."

Heidi finished her soda, and they stood up. "But. . . ."

"I mean it. It works." Cher grinned. "And someday the boys will grow up."

As they started toward the center of the mall, Cher gave her a quick hug. "Pretty soon you'll be as good-lookin' as I am."

This time it was Heidi's turn to smile.

TO TALK ABOUT

▶What causes some girls to develop before others?

▶ Is there a right or a wrong time as to when a girl's body changes? Why or why not?

▶When kids tease others about their appearance, what does it show about the kid doing the teasing?

▶Both boys and girls often experience teasing about the way they look. (Your ears, your nose, the hair on your arms, or whatever.) In what ways have you learned to handle teasing?

▶Did the kids stop teasing you, or did you learn to live with it? Give an example. Why can learning how to live with something seem like a miracle?

▶How do you think God feels about your body and the way He made it? Why?

Whoever is wise, let him understand these things. Whoever is intelligent, let him listen. For the paths of the Lord are true and right, and good men walk along them (Hosea 14:9, TLB)

Jesus, it's not fun being different, but help me learn how to handle teasing. Help me remember that You know how it feels to be different. Thanks for loving me just the way I am.

FRENCH FRIES
AND LOVE

Book in hand, Jill flopped down on her bed and rolled onto her stomach. Mom had said she could bring her friend Kim home from school. It'd been fun having time together.

Now Kim leaned forward. "Is that your sister's book about dating?"

Jill flipped pages. "Yep. Here's where we left off." She began reading aloud. "Love isn't something that just happens. You choose who you love or don't love."

Kim stopped her. "Just a minute. What does that mean?"

"Let me finish," answered Jill. She continued reading. "Some people say, 'I fell in love. I just couldn't help myself.' But...."

Again Kim interrupted. "That's true. I do fall in love. If I like a boy, I like him. And right now I like Willy. What's so bad about that?"

"What's *good* about it?" asked Jill.

She went back to the book. "Some people say, 'I fell in love. I just couldn't help myself.' But early in every relationship there's a moment of choice, whether we think about it or not. We decide, 'I'm not interested in that boy as more than just a friend.' Or we tell ourselves, 'I like that boy. I hope he becomes my special friend.'"

"That's true," said Kim. "I decide all right. When I meet a boy I know real fast if he's the one for me. I don't know why my mom won't let me start dating."

Jill sighed. "Kim, you're missing the whole point of the book. We can know a lot of people and be nice to them. But the book says there're times when we should choose to *not* become special friends with someone—especially someone we might date. We might wind up getting hurt."

"Oh, phooey," said Kim. "You choose your friends, and I'll choose mine." Then she grinned. "Of course, you can keep choosing *me!*"

Jill rolled off the bed and stood up. "Come on. Mom left money, and she said we could bike to get burgers. She won't be home for awhile."

A short time later the girls slid into a booth. As Kim picked up her first French fry, she glanced out the window. "Look! Willy and Chris!"

Jill's eyes lit up. As she and Kim watched, Chris and Willy bought hamburgers, then headed over to sit with the girls.

Moments later, Willy tugged a strand of Kim's hair. "Hey, kid, how you doing?" Pushing his baseball cap to a cocky angle, he smiled lazily. "Did you see me at the game Saturday? Got the best hit of the whole team."

Kim nodded, her eyes shining. "You were terrific, Willy."

"Well, next game I'll do even better. Just keep your eye on ol' Willy."

Chris coughed and winked at Jill, knowing how she felt about Willy's bragging.

Jill smiled. "You got a hit that brought in two runs," she said to Chris. But instead of bragging about it, he just grinned.

As the four of them ate, Jill started thinking. "That's what the book was talking about! I can choose to like Chris, or choose to like Willy. And I like more things about Chris than about Willy. A whole lot more!"

Soon the boys finished eating and started to leave. Chris turned back. "See you at the church carwash, Jill."

Jill waved, then watched as Chris headed out. Ahead of him, Willy and a young mother reached the

double doors at the same time. She held a baby in her right arm, and her left hand clung to a little boy.

The mother leaned into one door to push it open. Just then, Willy rushed ahead through the other. Caught off balance, the mother almost fell. The next moment, Willy's door swung back, catching the toddler in the face.

As he let out a yowl, Jill jumped up. "Oh, did you

see that?" She rushed forward to help, but Chris was there ahead of her. Pulling the little boy to one side, he started comforting him.

Still holding the baby, the mother knelt down beside them, looking grateful.

When the boy stopped crying and looked up at Chris, Jill breathed a sigh of relief. As she watched, Chris helped the mother and children to their car.

Jill went back and sat down with Kim. "Watch out for number one, that's Willy!"

"Are you kidding, Jill?" asked Kim. "It was an accident. Willy didn't mean for them to get hurt."

"He was the *cause* of them getting hurt! Did you see him push ahead? He's the rudest person I've ever known!"

"You're just jealous because he didn't pay attention to you."

Jill's anger felt like lava pouring out of a volcano. But Kim's thoughts had already raced on.

"Isn't he dreamy?"

"Who?"

"Willy, of course! Who else?"

Jill groaned. "Kim, does Willy ever go to church?"

Kim thought for a moment. "No, I guess not. What does that have to do with it?"

"You know that book we were reading? It talks about choosing Christians for our special friends."

"What's the big deal? I'm not going to *marry* Willy.

I just *like* him. When I get old enough, maybe he'll ask me out."

"What if you always go with guys like Willy? All he thinks about is himself."

"But he's fun too. And he's a superstar. When I'm ready to get married, I'll find one that goes to church."

Jill didn't believe Kim. Yet she knew she couldn't change her mind. As she gathered up her food wrappers and tray, she thought ahead to the next afternoon. "I can hardly wait to see Chris again."

TO TALK ABOUT

▶From what you know about Chris and Willy, which boy do you respect the most? Why?

▶Which boy do you think would be most thoughtful of the girl he dates? Why?

▶Which girl, Jill or Kim, do you respect the most? Why?

▶Jesus can use our friendships as an opportunity for us to tell others about Him. Yet some kids think, "I'll go with that boy—or that girl—and I'll witness so that kid becomes a Christian." Do you think it actually works that way? Why or why not?

▶When you choose Christians for your closest friends, you meet other kids through them. Soon you know a whole group of Christian kids. Whether you're a boy or a girl, why is it important to know that?

▶When your parents let you start dating, why will it help you to date a Christian?

Don't be teamed with those who do not love the Lord, for what do the people of God have in common with the people of sin? How can light live with darkness? (2 Corinthians 6:14, TLB)

Jesus, please give me special friends who are Christians. Show me the good qualities in people so that when I date I know what to look for. If I get married someday, I want it to be to a Christian who loves You the way I do.

67

JASON'S CHOICE

Jason jumped down from the school bus, then looked back. Sure enough, Teresa was looking through the window. Jason waved good-bye to her.

Teresa waved back. Even through the glass, her smile lit up her soft brown eyes. "Wow! Is she ever super!" thought Jason for the hundredth time.

As he headed down the block, Kent and Del fell into step beside him. "Wanna come over for awhile?" asked Kent.

Jason remembered Dad's words. "I don't want you hanging around with those kids."

But when Dad didn't know, Jason did it anyway. He liked being with Kent and Del. Sure, sometimes they wanted him to do things he shouldn't, but. . . . "I can handle it," Jason thought.

Aloud he said, "Yeah, I'll stop for awhile." He knew why they were going to Kent's house. His mom would be working. No one would be home.

While they were shooting baskets, Del and Kent started talking about the girls at school. As they went from one girl to another, the jokes got worse. Jason felt uncomfortable.

"But what can I do?" he thought. "If I say anything, they'll laugh at me, too."

Then Kent started talking about Teresa.

"That's not true!" answered Jason.

"Hey, what's with you?" asked Kent, tossing the ball to Del.

"She's a nice girl!" answered Jason. "Quit talking about her."

"Jason loves Teresa! Jason loves Teresa!" called out Kent in a singsong chant.

Del joined in. "Jason loves Teresa!"

"Aw, get off my back!" Jason shouted.

Kent threw down the basketball. "Come on, I wanna show you something."

Jason and Del followed Kent into the garage. Stacked along one wall were newspapers and magazines for a paper drive. Kent dug down in one pile and pulled out a bunch of magazines.

"Take a look at these, you guys," he said. "I found

some of my old man's magazines."

Jason picked one up and felt sick all the way through. "No wonder they talk the way they do," he thought. Quickly he put the magazine down. "I have to get home," he said.

"Who're you kiddin'?" answered Kent. "You don't have to go for another hour yet. What's the matter? You chicken? No one will catch us."

Just then a picture of Teresa's face, smiling through the bus window, flashed through Jason's mind.

"Hey, what are you, religious or something?" asked Kent.

"He's a Jesus freak," called out Del.

"I don't want to read that junk," Jason said, heading out the garage door.

"What are you, a pansy? You'd like the pictures."

Their jeers followed Jason as he started down the street. For a moment he slowed down, knowing they wouldn't forget this. "Next time I see 'em they'll be mad," he thought. "Maybe they won't be my friends anymore." Thinking about that, Jason stopped.

For a moment he stood at the side of the street, looking back. "I don't want to think that way about girls," he decided.

He started out again and then remembered. "Tomorrow I'll see Teresa again." This time he kept on going. He didn't look back.

TO TALK ABOUT

▶What kind of magazines were in Kent's garage?

▶The word *pornography* refers to writing and pictures that make sex dirty. How do you think pornographic magazines had affected Kent and Del?

▶If someone spends a lot of time thinking sinful thoughts, how will it affect the way that person acts? If someone thinks about good things, how will it affect the way that person acts? See Psalm 119:11 and 2 Timothy 2:22 for clues.

▶Why did Jason refuse to look at the magazines? Why will that help him keep a better attitude toward girls?

▶Jason had to choose whether he wanted to be one of the guys or do what he felt was right. He made a good choice, even though it made his friends tease him. When have you needed to make a choice, even though it was hard? How did you feel about yourself after you made a good choice?

▶If you have a problem with thinking thoughts that you know are sinful, you can ask Jesus to forgive you. Then ask Him to make your mind clean. Next put good thoughts into your mind and spirit. One of the best ways to do that is to memorize Bible verses. Whenever you have wrong thoughts, recall those verses. Repeat them to yourself. One good verse might be Philippians 4:8. What are some other verses that could help you?

▶ If you have trouble with your thought life, it also helps to get regular exercise and do things that take your mind off negative or sinful thoughts. What are some things you can do with kids at church? What activities can you take part in at school?

May my spoken words and unspoken thoughts be pleasing to you, O Lord my Rock and my Redeemer. (Psalm 19:14, TLB)

Jesus, I want to have clean words and clean thoughts. Help me to store Your words in my heart so they keep me back from sin.

ARE BOYS REALLY BETTER?

Christy slid onto the tractor seat. It felt good to curl her fingers around the large steering wheel. When she first started driving the tractor, she'd been afraid of it. Now it had become her friend.

"What a great day!" she thought. From a cloudless sky, the sun beat down on the road stretching out before her. Haying was fun on mornings like this. If the weather held, they'd get everything in before rain edged up over the horizon.

For a moment, the breeze lifted Christy's hair, tossing it in her face. Pulling it back out of her eyes, she wished she'd drawn the long strands into a pony tail. Shifting the tractor into gear, she took a quick look at the hay wagon behind her.

"Either sit down or hang on!" she called.

Her two cousins waved, and each slung an arm around the posts at the front of the wagon. Todd and Kenny were there for the summer. Christy had to admit she was getting tired of their company.

"Why does Dad keep asking them back every June?" she wondered. "They're almost my age, yet they don't do nearly the work."

As they moved onto the gravel road, stones kicked up around the tractor. A trail of dust billowed behind the wagon. Soon Christy drove into a field.

Dad was there ahead of her, using the baler. Christy watched as one bale after another shot up and then back, falling into the nearly full wagon behind Dad's tractor.

Once again Christy twisted around to check on her cousins. They were wrestling. Todd had Kenny pinned dangerously close to the edge of the wagon.

"Hey, you guys, quit it!" shouted Christy. "If I start up suddenly, you'll fall off."

Turning back, she saw Dad motioning to her. "Get a move on!" his arms seemed to say.

Christy pulled up behind Dad's baler. "What took so long?" he asked. Without waiting for an answer, Dad hopped down to unhitch Christy's wagon. She set the brake and went to help, but Dad was still impatient. "You should have been a boy," he grumbled.

"You never work the way a boy would."

Christy felt hot tears coming into her eyes. Often she had protested, saying, "I can't help the way I was born, Dad." Instead of trying again, she leaned down, hiding her face as she hooked the chains under the hitch.

All day long, as Christy drove between field and barn, her thoughts were elsewhere. Like snapshots, one memory after another seemed to appear before her eyes.

Mom telling her, "We didn't have a girl's name picked out for you. You were going to be a Christopher instead of Christine."

A neighbor saying, "When you were only three years old, you wanted to do a boy's work. One day I saw you trying to carry large stones for your dad."

By mid-afternoon Christy was tired of thinking about the way things were. "I've tried and tried," she thought. "But does it do any good? Does Dad love me at all? I just want to please him."

That day, for the first time all summer, they finished work early. Mom had a good supper fixed. As everyone dug into the roast beef and potatoes, Dad looked at Todd and Kenny. "Want to go for a swim when we're done eating?"

"You betcha!" they exclaimed and started eating faster. Watching them, Christy thought about how good her warm, dusty body would feel diving into the cool water. She imagined the water closing over her head, and the pull of her muscles in the long swim back from the raft.

"It'd feel so great," she thought. "And it'd be fun, just being with Dad. Maybe just once. . . ."

"Dad, can I go too?" she asked.

"Nope, this is only for boys," he answered.

Like the rush of water ready to spill over a dam, Christy felt anger and despair rise within her. She wanted to cry out, "I'm worth something, Dad! I'm worth something, even though I'm a girl!"

But she had said those things before, and it hadn't helped.

Without a word, Christy stood up and carried her dishes to the sink. As she set them down, she turned and looked back at Dad, still sitting at the table. "But I'm gonna try once more!" she thought.

Soon Mom finished her coffee and went to find the boys' swimsuits. Todd and Kenny left to change clothes, and Christy sat down across the table from Dad.

"I want to tell you something," she said, facing Dad squarely. "I want to tell you how I feel."

Dad looked at Christy, as though surprised at her tone of voice.

A nervous feeling started in Christy's stomach, but she kept on. "All my life you've wanted me to be something I can't be. I'm not a boy. I'm a girl! I can't help that. But you make me feel I'm no good!"

Dad stared at Christy as though not believing what he was hearing. For the first time in her life, Christy stared back instead of looking at the floor.

This time Dad was the first to look away. As he set down his coffee cup, his hand shook, and the cup rattled in the saucer.

For a long moment Dad sat there without speaking, his head bowed. When he finally spoke, his voice sounded strange and far away. "I'm sorry, Christy," he said, still looking down. "That's what my ma and pa always told me. No matter what I did, they'd say, 'You're no good. You're no good.'"

Dad's broad shoulders began to shake, and Christy felt scared. She'd never seen Dad cry before. When he looked up, there were tears in his eyes.

"I heard it so often, I've always thought I'm no good. I've passed that feeling on to you."

Christy searched his eyes, wondering what to say. The pain in Dad's face was like the pain she'd felt all these years.

Dad spoke again. "I'm sorry, Christy. I'm so sorry."

In the quiet room Christy heard the ticking of the clock. The moment seemed to stretch out forever. But at last she knew what to do.

Standing up, Christy slowly circled the table. For the first time since she was a little girl, she gave Dad a hug.

TO TALK ABOUT

▶On farms, men and women often work together, sometimes doing much of the same work. Because of that, did Christy's dad have a real reason for wanting a boy? What clues tell you that he valued boys more than girls?

▶Because of the way he treated her, how did Christy feel about being a girl? How do you think God feels about her being a girl?

▶Why did it take courage for Christy to tell her dad what was wrong?

▶When Christy's dad talked about feeling no good, he said, "I've passed that feeling on to you." What does it mean to pass a feeling on to someone else?

▶Do you think Christy's dad will change in the way he treats her? Why or why not?

▶If her dad doesn't change, what kind of people could Christy talk with to get encouragement? Why is it important that Christy knows she's valuable exactly the way she is?

▶Sometimes it's not possible to change the way people treat us. Yet if we ask God, He can help us change the way we feel about ourselves. Are there ways in which you hurt because of the way people have treated you? You can talk with an adult you trust about it. That person can pray with you and ask God to show you good things about yourself.

▶In God's sight is your being a boy or a girl ever an accident? How do you know?

You created every part of me; you put me together in my mother's womb. (Psalm 139:13, GNB)

Lord, I thank You for creating me just the way I am. Help me remember that You're the One who decided whether I'm a boy or a girl. Help me value the person I am now and the person I can become as I grow older. Give me the healing I need.

THE RIGHT TOUCH

"It's for you, Dad," said Renee, as she held out the phone.

Dad pulled himself out of his favorite chair. "Keep down the noise," he said. "I'll take it in the other room."

As Dad talked on the phone, Renee looked around the circle that was her family. Mom sat next to a light, knitting a sweater. Amy played on the floor, dressing her favorite doll. In another corner Terry and Paul raced cars together. In that moment Renee thought about how much all of them meant to her.

Dad returned, a grin lighting his face. "Guess what?" he asked.

"You're going out of town on business," said Paul.

"We're going to move again," guessed Terry.

Mom looked up and her gaze met Dad's. Whatever she saw there erased two worry lines between her eyes.

"Try again," said Dad.

"You have a meeting this weekend," said Amy.

"No, no, no," answered Dad.

"You're all guessing wrong," said Renee. "The way Dad looks it must be something good. Oh, I know! You won the sales contest."

"Right!" Dad's eyes twinkled. "I won the trip for two. Your mother and I can fly to California, stay in a motel right near the beach, go sightseeing, and enjoy ourselves for a week."

"Grrreeat, Dad!" said Renee.

Dad held up his hand. "Wait a minute, wait a minute. I'm not through yet. Your mom and I had a vacation together four months ago. So I asked my boss if I could make a trade. What if I drove to California instead of flying? And what if I stayed in a less expensive motel? Could I take all of you instead?"

"Really, Dad?" A chorus went up. "We could really all go?"

Dad grinned and went into his deepest voice. "He said, 'Fine, Jennings, fine. I'm all for family vacations myself.'"

Everyone jumped up. Amy squealed. Paul took a flying leap and landed in Dad's arms. Terry followed. Suddenly the room filled with laughter and hugs.

"What a good feeling it is to be a family," thought Renee as she hugged Dad and Mom, Amy, and her brothers. "What a good feeling it is to love each other."

The celebration continued around her, but in the next instant Renee's happiness dimmed. "We'll be going back to California," she thought. "We'll see Uncle Henry again."

Like a picture in Renee's mind came the last time they'd visited him. She tried to brush aside the memory, but couldn't. She thought about Uncle Henry, and how he tried to touch the private parts of her body. Even now, Renee felt uncomfortable just thinking about it.

"Why is it fun having my family hug me?" Renee asked herself. "And why is it awful when Uncle Henry does?" Once before, when she was a little girl, he made her feel uncomfortable. Then he said not to tell anyone.

Quietly Renee sat down next to Mom. Mom looked at her and asked, "What's the matter, Renee?"

"Should I tell her?" Renee debated within herself. "Should I say something about Uncle Henry? Or should I pretend everything is okay?"

Mom spoke again. "If there's something wrong, telling me can make a difference."

"Is that really true?" Renee wondered. "Would Mom make a difference?"

She hesitated, thinking things over. "What if

Mom doesn't believe me?"

A moment later everyone but Mom scattered to other parts of the house. Renee sat on the floor thinking. Finally she decided to give it a try.

"When we go to California, will we see Uncle Henry again?"

"Probably," said Mom. "Why?"

"He makes me feel creepy," answered Renee.

"What do you mean?" asked Mom.

"He made me promise I wouldn't tell anyone."

"Then I think it's important that you tell me. Sometimes when adults tell you *not* to say anything, it's because something is wrong. That's different from being a tattletale."

For a little longer Renee was quiet. "That's the way it felt," she said. "Like something was wrong. It didn't feel good. Last summer, when we were alone once, he touched me in private places."

A flash of anger crossed Mom's face. "I'm glad you told me," she said. "Your body is very special, and it belongs to you. Uncle Henry shouldn't touch you that way. Dad and I will make sure it doesn't happen again."

"But what should I do if he tries?"

"You can say, 'NO!' in the biggest voice you've got. You can say, 'I don't want to be touched that way.' But you've already done the best thing, you've told me. And I promise you, it won't happen again."

Renee stood up. Already she felt better—as though a great big bag of stones had rolled off her back. Telling Mom really *did* make a difference.

TO TALK ABOUT

▶Why is it important that Renee told her mom about the way Uncle Henry treated her?

▶If Renee's mom hadn't believed what she said, what other adults could she have talked with? Think of people Renee would know from her family, church, or school.

▶Good touch makes kids feel loved, happy, and right inside themselves. What are some times when you've enjoyed being hugged by your family, relatives, or friends? How did you feel afterward?

▶Bad touch makes kids feel confused, sad, ashamed, or scared. Bad touch may involve the parts of your body covered by your swimsuit. What can you tell a person who touches you in a way you don't like?

▶What if someone offered you some money or candy and then tried to hug you? Do you think that would be good touch or bad touch? Why?

▶If you feel uncomfortable about the way a person touches you, you always have the right to tell someone about it. How can the right adult change what is happening?

▶It's important for you to obey adults when they ask

you to do something. But it's different if an adult asks you to do something wrong. Then you should say, NO! or run away, and then ask the right person for help. The Bible tells us about Daniel and Esther. What did they do when people tried to do wrong things to them? Did they allow the people to win, or did they try to change what was happening? How? What miracles did God give Daniel and Esther? (See Daniel 6:10-11,21-23; and Esther 4:15-16, 7:3, 8:11.)

The LORD keeps close watch over the whole world, to give strength to those whose hearts are loyal to him.
(2 Chronicles 16:9, GNB)

Thank You, Jesus, for all the times I've learned Your love because my family and friends hug me in the right way. If I'm ever uncomfortable with the way people touch me, help me to say NO! and talk to the right grownup. Thank You that telling the right person makes a difference in what happens to me.

LIKE A PORCUPINE

Colleen slammed the door of her locker. "What do you mean I'll get a bad grade?"

Karen took a step back. "Well, don't get mad at me. I'm just telling you what Mr. Lindquist said. For each day your paper's late it gets marked down."

"Well, bug off," answered Colleen. "I don't wanna hear about it."

"Hey, come on. . . ."

"I said bug off! You sound just like my mom."

Karen tried again. "Hey, we're friends, remember? I was just trying to help. What's really bugging you?"

But Colleen was halfway down the hall. As she reached the outside door, she thought about the hurt look in Karen's eyes.

Colleen turned and looked back. Karen had started in the other direction. Instead of going after her, Colleen shrugged her shoulders and headed out the door.

Fifteen minutes later she dropped her books on the kitchen table. Mom was at the sink, peeling potatoes. Seeing Colleen, Mom tried to give her a hug. But Colleen brushed Mom aside.

When Mom asked, "Did you have a nice day?" Colleen answered, "Fine, fine." As soon as she finished her cookies and milk, she headed upstairs to her room.

Half an hour later Mom knocked on her door.

"Whadda you want?" Colleen answered.

"May I come in?" asked Mom through the door.

"Well, I s'pose," Colleen called back. "It's your house."

Slowly the door opened, and Mom came in. It was hard finding a place to sit down, but she managed. Picking up a pile of clothes, she cleared off a chair.

For a long moment Mom was silent. Finally she asked, "How'd your day go?"

"Whadda you think?" answered Colleen from where she sprawled on the bed.

Mom tried again. "How do you feel about how your day went?"

It was like opening a faucet. All the bad things that had happened poured out. Starting from the moment she left home until she got back again, Colleen told everything that had gone wrong.

Mom listened without speaking. Only once, when Colleen stopped, did she say, "I don't know what you mean. Will you explain it again?"

At last Colleen finished with the words, "Even my best friend doesn't understand. Even Karen. . . ." Breaking off, she stopped, afraid the tears would come.

Mom's voice was gentle. "Colleen, how do you feel on the inside?"

"Whadda you mean?"

"On the inside. You told me all the bad things that happened to you today. But how do you *feel* about what happened?"

"Well. . . ." Colleen thought for a moment. "I feel mad. I feel dumb. I feel like I'm not worth anything. I wanna hit back. I wanna get even."

"You feel like a porcupine?" asked Mom.

For the first time Colleen almost smiled. She knew what Mom meant. Last summer they'd seen a porcupine cross a country road. Its quills stuck out all over. The end of those quills had barbs that stayed in whatever flesh they touched. Whoever was on the receiving end of a porcupine's quills felt pain.

"Yep," she answered. "Like a porcupine." For the first time she wondered, "Is it the things around me that are so bad? Or the way I feel about them?" Right then Colleen felt ready to stick quills in everyone.

91

"I'm glad you told me how you feel," said Mom. "You know, the feelings you have aren't right or wrong. But you make the choice whether you're going to let those feelings control you."

Mom grinned. "Or do you want to stay like a porcupine? What's important is learning how to handle your feelings in a good way. Like right now. Why do you feel so grumpy?"

For a long time Colleen didn't answer. Mom waited. Finally, Colleen spoke in a low voice. "I guess I woke up that way. I was mad at you last night, and I felt the same way when I woke up."

"Can you tell me some of the things that made you mad?" asked Mom.

"Sure," said Colleen, jumping at the chance. As she sat up and faced Mom, her words poured out. "Sometimes you expect too much of me. Sometimes you treat me like a little kid."

As Colleen continued, Mom listened without speaking. Once she flinched, and a hurt look entered her eyes. In a moment it disappeared.

When at last Colleen finished, Mom said, "Tonight after supper, let's make a list. We'll decide what both of us feel would be the right amount of work. You tell me what you feel you can handle, okay?"

Mom paused. "Something else is happening. Things that never used to upset you bother you now. Sometimes you feel grumpy or really mad. Other times

92

you're at the top of a mountain. Everything in the whole world is wonderful. Your moods go up, down, up, down."

Colleen thought about it. "Yep, you're right."

Mom went on. "Your body is changing. The way you think and feel about things is changing. Some of the things you used to like doing seem like kid stuff now. Do you know what I mean by saying that your emotions swing back and forth?"

Colleen nodded. "My moods go up and down."

"That's something that happens to both boys and girls your age. As a girl, you may notice the feeling more just before your period."

Colleen felt relieved, knowing that was true. "Do you have up and down days, too?"

"All of us do," answered Mom. "Sometimes we know what causes good and bad feelings. A sunny day or bright colors—they make most of us feel better. As far as feeling bad, there're lots of reasons. Someone may say something, or you're tired, or. . . ."

"Sometimes I don't know why I feel this way."

"Sometimes you *won't* know why," answered Mom. "That's okay. But grumpy moods are something all of us need to fight."

Just then Colleen remembered Karen and the hurt look in her eyes. "I wonder how she's gonna feel about me tomorrow," Colleen thought.

"Do you think you'd feel better about yourself if

you learned some ways to handle your moods?" asked Mom. When Colleen didn't answer, Mom stood up. "Why don't you think about it for awhile?"

As Mom headed for the door, Colleen wanted to reach out for a hug, the way she used to. Instead she said, "I didn't think you'd understand."

For a long time Colleen lay on her bed thinking. The next day, when she saw Karen, Colleen was still thinking. But Karen didn't look too happy to see her.

In that moment, Colleen felt ashamed. "She's my friend," Colleen told herself. "But she doesn't know how I'll treat her—if I'm gonna be mad or gonna be nice."

Knowing that didn't make Colleen feel very good. "I guess I'd better do something about it," she thought.

TO TALK ABOUT

▶What do you think Colleen did about the way she'd treated Karen?

▶What does it mean to feel like a porcupine?

▶Why was it important for Colleen to talk about how she felt? Are feelings right or wrong? What *is* right or wrong?

▶What if Colleen's mom had said, "You shouldn't feel that way?" What do you think Colleen would have done?

▶When Colleen comes home from school in a bad

mood, she can warn her family by saying, "I feel . . ." and finish the sentence with a feeling word like *mad, upset,* or *cranky.* Pretend you're Colleen: What would you say?

▶What does it mean to "nurse a grudge"? Why can that be a difficult way to live? How did it help Colleen to express her anger at her mom?

▶In what ways can Colleen learn to handle her down moods? You can help her by finishing these sentences:

> If she's swamped with homework, she can say, "I feel. . . ."
>
> If she's angry, she can say, "I feel. . . ."
>
> If she's hurt, she can say, "I feel. . . ."

▶To handle moods it also helps to do other things.

> If Colleen is cranky because she's tired, she can. . . .
>
> If she wants to be alone for awhile, she can. . . .
>
> If she needs to forgive someone, she can. . . .
>
> Instead of continuing to think about how bad she feels, Colleen can. . . .
>
> If she needs exercise, she can. . . .

▶In what ways do you get rid of your down moods?

▶Sometimes people say, "Don't go out the door when you're angry." Why can that be a good idea?

▶Is the way you think about yourself based on your feelings or on God's love? What difference does that make?

If you are angry, don't sin by nursing your grudge. Don't let the sun go down with you still angry—get over it quickly; for when you are angry you give a mighty foothold to the devil. (Ephesians 4:26-27, TLB)

Jesus, You know my body is changing. Often I have up and down moods. Help me handle my moods in the right way. I want to be a fun person to be around.

MONTY GOES FISHING

Early morning sunlight sparkled on the water as Monty headed the boat away from the dock. Soon he and Dad reached their favorite part of the lake. Monty slowed the outboard motor to trolling speed. Picking up his fishing rod, he baited the hook.

As he cast out his line, he turned to Dad. "Can I ask you a question?"

"Sure," said Dad.

"Well. . . . What does it mean when a kid says someone is gay?"

Dad put a minnow on his line. "Gay is a word people use to describe *homosexuality*. Why do you wonder about it?"

"From kids talking, and people on TV. Sometimes they talk about gay rights. What does gay mean?"

"Let's go back to Creation," Dad said. "When God created man and woman, He made them in such a way that they feel attracted to one another. As a man and woman get to know each other, that attraction may change into love. If it does, they may want to get married—like your mom and I did."

Dad dropped his line over the side of the boat. "God also created us so we have friendships. A boy has a friendship with another boy, or a girl has a friendship with another girl. Take Ben, for instance. What do you like about having him for a friend?"

Monty thought for a moment. "Well, we do stuff together. We play catch, and help each other with homework. We walk to the bus. Is that what you mean?"

"Yep. You count on each other, don't you? You don't depend on each other so much that you don't do things with other kids, but you help each other out.

"Remember when you got upset because your dog died? You talked with Mom and me, but after awhile you took off. You went over to Ben's. You shot baskets with him. You talked. And when you came back, you felt better. You knew he understood."

Monty nodded.

"That's a very good kind of relationship for you to have," said Dad. "And a girl can have a good relationship like that with another girl."

"Yeah," said Monty. "Only girls giggle and talk all the time."

Dad grinned. "It's also normal to have a good relationship between a mother and daughter or a father and son. We talk together like we're doing now, and your mom does the same with your sister. I'm not sure all they talk about, but. . . ."

"Girl stuff."

"And that's important, isn't it?" asked Dad. He reeled in his line. "Just like it's important that I talk with you."

"I know some guys at school who act kind of girlish," said Monty. "They don't like sports or fun things like that. And they carry their books like girls. Richie bugs them, and calls them gay. Can you tell someone's gay by the way he walks or talks?"

"Calling kids names or teasing them so they feel hurt isn't a good way to treat *anyone*," answered Dad. "Whether someone likes sports, or doesn't like sports, doesn't have anything to do with it. And how a boy carries his books doesn't make him gay.

"It's not a good idea to decide what someone's like sexually by the way they look on the outside. Sometimes we can guess things about people by how they dress or act, but we might be wrong, too. Maybe it's better not to guess at all than to think the wrong thing about someone."

99

Dad checked his minnow and let out his line again. "But it's also important to know that if a boy or a man asks you to do things that make you feel uneasy, you need to say no."

"What do you mean?" asked Monty. "What if guys hug each other?"

"A lot of men hug each other, just like a lot of women hug each other. Usually it's a way of saying hi or 'I'm glad to see you.' That's normal.

"What I'm talking about is wrong touch," Dad went on. "When we're together, and you do something I like, I slap you on the back and say, 'That's great, Monty!' Or, 'Good catch!' Or, 'Great play!' We wrestle together. Or I put my arm around your shoulders and hug you. That's normal. But people who are called homosexual have a sexual attraction for each other. Two men or two women have a close sexual relationship."

"Joey's big brother said . . ." Monty stopped and then tried again. "Joey's big brother said that he's gay. He even said, 'God made me that way.'"

"The Bible doesn't tell us God made people that way," answered Dad. "The Bible says homosexual behavior is sinful. And sin separates people from God. God loves everyone so much He wouldn't create them in a way that would separate them from Him.

"Maybe Joey's brother had a homosexual experience," Dad went on. "Sometimes that happens, and a lot of kids think that if they have one experience, that means they're gay. It doesn't mean that. They can ask God's forgiveness and choose to leave that behavior behind. All of us need to make choices about how we're going to act sexually. God will help us with those choices."

Just then Monty felt a strong tug on his line. Cutting the motor, he set the hook, then let the fish play a bit before reeling it in. In a few minutes a walleye came alongside the boat.

Dad slid the net under the fish just as it broke from the water. "Hey, look at that!"

Monty grinned. "Not bad, huh? Bet it'll weigh in at four pounds!"

It was the biggest catch of the day.

TO TALK ABOUT

▶Why was the fishing time a good opportunity for Monty to talk with his dad?

▶Why is a friendship between two boys or between two girls a good thing? Give your own ideas, then look for more clues in the story of David and Jonathan (1 Samuel 20).

▶When does a friendship between two people of the same sex become wrong?

▶The word *homo* means "the same." What does the word *homosexual* mean?

▶What does the Bible say about homosexual behavior? (See Romans 1:18-32.)
▶Jesus loves all of us, but He hates the sins we commit. What should our attitude be toward ourselves and others who sin?

Yes, all have sinned; all fall short of God's glorious ideal; yet now God declares us "not guilty" of offending him if we trust in Jesus Christ, who in his kindness freely takes away our sins. (Romans 3:23-24, TLB)

Thank You, Jesus, that You love everyone and died on the cross for all of us. Thank You that You forgive everyone who asks for Your forgiveness. I want to have friendships that please You. Help me to make good choices.

COUNTRY COUSIN

That morning Jenny had come into the city on the train. Jenny lived on a farm and hadn't seen her cousin Erica for over two years. Now they'd have a whole week of fun together.

The first thing Jenny noticed was that Erica had changed since the last time she'd seen her. "Wow!" Jenny thought. "Does she ever look cute." Jenny especially liked Erica's designer jeans.

That first afternoon they were off to a good start. Some boys dropped over to see Erica. Jenny especially liked Tim. As he left he called out, "See you at the party, Jenny!"

Erica's friends from school had planned a party for that evening. Jenny could hardly wait. As soon as the boys left, she followed Erica upstairs to figure out what to wear.

Jenny's half-open suitcase lay on the floor of Erica's bedroom. As Jenny started taking out her clothes, Erica stopped her. "Wait a minute," she said.

Erica pulled open the door of her closet. Jenny had never seen such a full closet. Jeans, shirts, and dresses were packed in as tight as they could go. On the floor beneath the clothes lay a jumble of shoes.

"We're almost the same size," said Erica. "Maybe I've got something you can wear."

"Grrreat!" thought Jenny. She hardly dared hope. "If I dress like Erica, maybe Tim will really like me."

Erica started at one end of the closet, pulling out shirts and then jeans. One by one Jenny tried them on. She liked one pair of jeans especially much.

Erica walked around her. "Nope," she said. "They're too loose."

"That's how I always wear 'em," answered Jenny.

But Erica kept looking. Soon she came up with another pair. "Try these. They're designers and fit better."

Jenny had all she could do to pull them on. She felt like she'd put her legs into tight steel buckets. Drawing in her breath, she managed to pull up the zipper.

Erica inspected her again. "Yep. They're perfect. That's how they're supposed to fit."

Jenny felt uncomfortable. "I can hardly breathe. How am I supposed to sit down?" she wondered. Yet she didn't dare ask Erica. More than anything, she wanted to fill out her jeans the way Erica did.

"Yep," said Erica, walking around Jenny once more. "Now you look like one of us."

"Well, then it's worth it," Jenny told herself. "That's what I want—to look like a city girl."

But when Jenny saw herself in the mirror, she felt uneasy. "I'm glad Mom and Dad won't see me," she thought. "They'd be upset." Aloud she said, "You're sure I won't split 'em?"

Erica laughed as though that was the funniest thing she'd ever heard.

Jenny pushed her uneasiness away, thinking, "It'll be fun looking as cute as Erica."

Soon it was time to leave, and the two girls set off down the street. The party was only two blocks away, at Anne's house.

As Jenny and Erica waited to cross a street, a car wheeled around the corner. The driver honked and waved. Jenny waved back.

Brakes squealed, and the driver backed up the car. Three boys leaned out of the windows to talk. They looked at least five years older then Jenny and Erica.

Jenny hung back, letting Erica do all the talking. At first Jenny felt shy, then uncomfortable, then almost scared. There was just something about these boys she really didn't like.

Finally one of them asked, "Wanna ride somewhere?"

Erica shook her head. "Nah, but thanks. We're going to a party just down the street."

As the boys pulled away, they asked Erica's name. Revving up the engine, the driver called out, "Well, see ya around!"

"You mean you didn't know them?" asked Jenny as the car pulled away from the curb.

"Of course not! Never saw them before in my life!"

"Then why did you talk to them?"

Erica looked at Jenny as though she thought that was the most stupid question in the world. "Hey, you're the one who waved."

"At home we wave at everyone," answered Jenny. "But when they honked, I thought you knew them. How come they stopped?"

Erica smirked. "They just liked the way we looked."

Jenny's heart thudded down to her toes. "So that's it!" she thought. "That's why she didn't want me wearing my own jeans."

Suddenly all the beautiful clothes in Erica's closet didn't mean very much. To Jenny they seemed like a bunch of junk—junk that made Erica look the wrong way.

"Sure, I want to look nice," thought Jenny. "I want to look like the other kids. But. . . ."

Jenny looked down at her skintight jeans and didn't like herself very much. She felt ashamed. She didn't like what she was saying through the clothes she wore. Then she thought about Tim and wanting to dress so he'd like her.

She breathed deep, and the button at her waist popped off. "Oh, wow! I can't go to the party this way."

"Aw, come on," answered Erica. "No one will notice. We'll find a pin when we get there."

In that split-second, Jenny knew it wouldn't work to explain to Erica. "Why don't you go to the party? I'll run back and take care of it."

"Welllll. . . ."

"I know where Anne's house is," said Jenny quickly. "I was there last time I visited you. Go on, and I'll catch up."

Before Erica could say another word, Jenny was off. As soon as she reached her cousin's bedroom, she pulled her best jeans from the suitcase and changed into them.

"It's not whether I live in the country or the city," she decided. "It's the kind of person I want to be."

For a moment she stood in front of the full-length mirror. "I look nice," she thought, feeling surprised.

When she reached the party, Tim had been looking around for her. Something in his grin gave him away.

"He likes me the way I am," thought Jenny.

TO TALK ABOUT

▶What did Jenny mean when she decided, "It's not whether I live in the country or the city. It's the kind of person I want to be"?

▶Whether you're a boy or a girl, how can clothes tell other people what kind of person you are?

▶What did Erica want to say through the way she dressed? What did Jenny want to say?

▶Why do most kids want to wear clothes that are the same as what other kids wear? What's the difference between wearing clothes that are in and clothes that give the wrong impression?

▶Why is it important that a Christian kid knows what he or she is saying through clothes?

▶Is it necessary to wear designer clothes in order to look nice? Why or why not?

▶If you make a choice like Jenny's or Erica's, what difference will it make in your life? How will it affect the kind of friends you have?

Be beautiful inside, with the lasting charm of a gentle and quiet spirit which is so precious to God. (1 Peter 3:4, TLB)

Jesus, I don't want to feel out of it with kids because of the way I dress. But I don't want to embarrass You either. Help me figure out how to dress in a way that honors You.

ALL MY PROBLEMS?

Trisha's church brought a busload of junior high and high school kids to hear a well-known Christian singer. As they emptied out of the bus, Trisha looked around.

Many of the older girls were with their boyfriends. Trisha watched them talking and laughing, looking sure of themselves. "I wish..." she thought, and then pushed the thought away.

She and her friend Kate followed Dave, the youth leader, and his wife, Sandy, into the auditorium. Seats were filling up fast. Dave turned and called out to the kids. "If we can't sit together, meet here at the end of the concert!"

Dave was right. They had to split up. Trisha and

Kate found themselves down near the front, two rows away from the other kids. Listening to the excited talk all around her, Trisha felt lonely again. "I bet if I had a boyfriend, I'd always feel good inside."

Soon the concert began. The music was great. Often the audience clapped along with the beat. Before long, Trisha forgot about herself. After a number of songs, the singer started telling about how he'd come to know Jesus.

As he described his past sinful life, Trisha felt uncomfortable. "Is there something wrong with me?" she wondered. "I don't have a very exciting testimony."

"Accept Jesus, and all your problems will be over," the singer said.

Now Trisha felt really confused. "I've already accepted Jesus, and I still have problems. Is there something I didn't do right?"

All around Trisha, kids began standing up and going forward. One minute Trisha wanted to join them; the next she felt like her feet wouldn't move. "Should I go forward again?" she wondered. "Didn't I really accept Jesus?"

For a long moment Trisha sat there. "I want to be a Christian, but I'm afraid to ask someone if I am. They'll think I'm dumb if I don't know."

Finally Trisha bowed her head. "Help me, Jesus," she prayed. "I really want to know where I'm at."

At the end of the concert, Trisha stood up and

slowly walked out. As she reached the outside door, she found Sandy. Trisha went over and stood beside her, hoping for a chance to talk, but scared to try.

For a long time Trisha stood there, watching kids pour out of the building. At last she worked up the courage to begin. "Sandy. . . ." Just then, someone grabbed Sandy's arm and started talking.

When they climbed on the bus, Trisha followed Sandy and sat down beside her. When the bus was dark, and they started back to the church, Trisha tried again. "Sandy, the singer said that if I became a Christian all my problems would be over. I . . . ."

"Are you confused? I'm glad you spoke up. He didn't say that right. He should have said, 'If you accept Jesus, He'll be *with you* in your problems.'"

"Whew!" thought Trisha, feeling like the Empire State Building had fallen off her back.

"Have you found that's true since you asked Jesus to be your Savior?"

"Well, I. . . ." Trisha thought about it for a moment. "Yeah, that's what it's been. But when the singer talked about how he was before he became a Christian, I thought. . . ."

As they passed under a streetlight, Trisha saw Sandy's grin. "You thought maybe you haven't been sinful enough? I know. When I hear some testimonies, I sometimes wonder that myself. But do you know something? You and I haven't gone through all the

113

suffering that comes with the kind of sin he talked about. We don't have to have a colorful past life. It's exciting to be a Christian now."

"He explained it in a different way—how to have salvation, I mean."

"Did you wonder if you needed to go forward again?" asked Sandy.

"Yeah," said Trisha in a quiet voice.

"Different speakers use different ways of explaining how to receive salvation," Sandy answered. "But when Dave and I prayed with you, you told Jesus you were sorry for your sins. You asked Him to be your Savior and Lord. That's what's important. When you did that, you became a Christian."

"But . . ." Trisha hesitated. "Sometimes I'm not sure. Sometimes I don't *feel* like I'm a Christian."

"Oh—but if you believed what you were saying when you prayed that prayer, you *are*. You can't depend on your feelings. You have to go by what God promised. Here. . . ."

Sandy dug in her purse and pulled out a small Bible and a pen flashlight. Finding the place she wanted, she handed the Bible and flashlight to Trisha. "Read this."

Just then, someone else asked Sandy a question. As she turned away, Trisha looked down and started reading. Suddenly the words were so real to Trisha that it seemed they'd been written just for her: "I write these things to you who believe in the name of the Son of God so that you may know that you have eternal life. . . ." In Sandy's Bible the word *know* was underlined.

Trisha let out a long breath, feeling as if she'd held it for the past hour. All around her, the bus was noisy, but in Trisha's spirit there was something steady and quiet. All the confusion she'd felt fell away.

Snapping off the flashlight, she sat there, not wanting to talk with anyone. But she prayed. "I asked You, Jesus," she told Him, without speaking aloud. "I asked You to be my Lord and Savior. So You *are!*"

In that moment, she had a surprising new thought. "It'll be fun to have a boyfriend someday, but. . . ."

No one had ever told her, but Trisha knew. "Jesus is the *only* One who can fill up *every* empty space inside."

TO TALK ABOUT

▶ Who is the only Person who gives you the power to change your life? How is this possible?
▶ Has Jesus promised to take away all your problems? How do you know?
▶ What does it mean to say, "Jesus will be *with you* in your problems"?
▶ In what way would you like to have Jesus help you?

Do you need to become a Christian? If so, you may
want to pray something like this: "Jesus, I'm sorry for
my sin. I believe You died on the cross for my sin, and
I ask You to forgive me. I ask You to be my Savior and
Lord. Thank You!"
▶ Or do you need to know that because you've asked,
you have received salvation? Why don't you read the
verses from 1 John 5:1,11-15 that Trisha read on the
bus?

Then, to help you remember what Jesus has done for
you and the choice you've made, write down your
prayer in the empty space below. Put the date and the
time and sign your name. If you're reading this alone,
why don't you tell another Christian about the prayer
you've prayed? It'll seem more real to you.

God said, "Do not be afraid—I will save you. I have
called you by name—you are mine. When you pass
through deep waters, I will be with you; your troubles
will not overwhelm you." (Isaiah 43:1-2, GNB)

Thank You, Jesus, for Your salvation for me. Thank
You that I don't have to depend on my feelings. Give
me the power to live by Your promises.

TONY'S QUESTION

As Tony entered the Christian school he attended, he thought about the news he'd seen that morning. The TV broadcast talked about three more people who had died of AIDS: a movie star, a little girl, and a twenty-two-year-old man.

Tony felt uneasy. All this talk about AIDS, and he didn't quite understand it. "Will I get it, too?" he wondered. He didn't like that idea one bit. As he started down the hall, he tried to push his uneasiness to the back of his mind.

Just the same, Tony's question quickly returned in health class later that day. Sometimes Mrs. Jensen's topics made him feel embarrassed. Often he wanted to disappear through the floor. But today she started out by saying, "I want to talk to you about AIDS."

Around Tony the kids stopped wiggling. The room grew quiet.

"*AIDS* stands for Acquired Immune Deficiency Syndrome. Those are big words. Can someone tell me what your *immune system* is?"

When Mrs. Jensen called on Tony, he felt glad they'd studied that. "It's what keeps me well," he said. "It's like having soldiers fight against the germs that try to make me sick."

"Good," said Mrs. Jensen. "Now let's say you were exposed to a cold. If your immune system worked well, what would happen?"

"I probably wouldn't get the cold," answered Tony.

"But what if your system *didn't* work?"

"I'd get sick."

Mrs. Jensen nodded. "A person with AIDS has a virus that attacks the immune system, so it doesn't work well. That person easily gets a cold, or flu, or anything else. And usually that person gets more sick, even with something like a cold, than someone who doesn't have AIDS."

Mrs. Jensen looked around the room. "Can someone tell me what happens to people with the AIDS virus?"

Several kids answered at once. "They die."

"Right," said Mrs. Jensen. "Sometimes people

120

carry the virus for many years before realizing they have it. They're called carriers and can infect other people, even though they don't know they're sick.

"Once someone gets the virus, there's no way to get rid of it. People die. Often they die from sicknesses they get because their immune system doesn't work in a normal way."

Inside Tony the scary feeling was back. "Will I get AIDS?" he asked himself again.

Mrs. Jensen went on. "There's no one who wants AIDS. So we need to know how people get it."

"Only gays get AIDS," blurted out a boy in the back of the room.

"It's true that many homosexuals do get it," answered Mrs. Jensen. "But the general population can also be affected."

Tony leaned forward to listen. This was exactly what he wanted to know.

"Some people have become sick with AIDS because of blood transfusions. Sometimes newborn babies have AIDS because their mothers were infected. But as you grow older, there'll be ways you can avoid getting AIDS."

Mrs. Jensen cleared her throat. "Some people get AIDS by sharing a dirty needle with someone else who shoots drugs. If you don't use drugs, you don't have to worry about getting AIDS that way.

"You can't get AIDS by touching or being around

121

someone who has the virus, but you can get it through sexual contact. We've already learned about sexual intercourse. It belongs in the relationship between a husband and wife. God doesn't want you to have sexual intercourse unless you're married. If you do get married, He wants you to be faithful to your husband or wife.

"If you and the person you marry wait with sexual intercourse until marriage, you offer each other a special gift. You've been faithful to the way God wants us to live. But you're also less likely to be carriers. You're less likely to get AIDS."

Mrs. Jensen looked slowly around the room. "Sometimes kids think they can get by with things. They think, 'Only once won't hurt.' But it's possible to get AIDS by having sex only once with an infected person.

"One of the most important things you can do is to live with Christian values. When others tempt you, say no. You'll be living the way God wants. You'll also be less likely to get AIDS."

Again Mrs. Jensen looked around the room. "Any questions?"

For a long moment Tony waited. "How would I feel if I got AIDS?" he wondered. "It'd be so awful to think, 'I'm gonna get worse and worse.'"

He was afraid to ask. But the idea of being that sick bothered him. Finally he raised his hand. "How should we act toward people who have AIDS?"

"That's an important question," answered Mrs. Jensen. "It shows you're doing some good thinking. We need to pray for people with AIDS. We need to be kind to them, the way we are to anyone who's sick and hurting. They need care and love like everyone else.

"But at the same time, we shouldn't say that the sexual lifestyle that spreads AIDS is okay. It's not. In the Bible God gives us clear guidelines for how He wants us to act. He tells us to be a holy people.

"Any more questions?" For a moment Mrs. Jensen waited. When no one spoke up, she said, "I have a quiz for you. I want to be sure all of you understand what I've told you."

As Tony picked up his pencil, he realized the scared feeling in his stomach was gone. "At least I have *some* choices," he thought. "I can choose how I want to live."

TO TALK ABOUT

▶What question started Tony thinking about AIDS?
▶In what ways do people get the virus that causes AIDS? Can you get AIDS just by being around someone who has it?
▶What happens to people with the AIDS virus? What happens to their immune system?
▶How should you treat people who have AIDS?

▶As you get older, you'll need to make a choice. How can saying no to sex outside of marriage lessen your risk of getting AIDS?

▶God wants all of us to be pure and devoted to Him. What does that mean? Does it mean you'll be perfect? Or does it mean you can ask forgiveness for your sin, be forgiven, and then live in a different way?

▶If you want to be like Jesus, how will the Holy Spirit help you?

May the God of peace himself make you entirely pure and devoted to God; and may your spirit and soul and body be kept strong and blameless until that day when our Lord Jesus Christ comes back again. God, who called you to become his child, will do all this for you, just as he promised. (1 Thessalonians 5:23-24, TLB)

Lord Jesus, I want to live the way You did when You were on earth. I want to live in a way that's clean and right and holy. Give me the power of Your Holy Spirit to help. Thank You!

DUSTY THINKS AHEAD

As his older brother ran onto the field, Dusty felt proud. "It's not every kid who has a football hero for a brother," he thought.

A junior in high school, Craig was already over six feet tall. With surprisingly broad shoulders for his age, he was the best receiving end Central had ever had.

As the team lined up, Dusty's friend Mark joined in the clapping and yelling. "Bet Craig will score again," Mark said.

The whistle blew, and the ball snapped into play. Time after time Craig was at exactly the right place at the right moment. As he caught the ball and completed a thirty-six-yard run, the crowd went wild.

Mark pounded Dusty's back. "Wow! Look at him!

He's so great now. What'll he be like as a senior?"

Around Dusty, the people started leaning forward or turning around. Everyone said the same thing. "What a great brother you have!"

"I know it!" Dusty called back, a wide grin on his face. But something inside started to hurt.

During a lull, he turned around, looking for Mom and Dad in the stands. Dad's face was alive with excitement. Mom had a crease between her eyebrows. Dusty knew what she was thinking. Before every game she'd say, "I hope Craig doesn't get hurt."

Dad also hoped Craig would be okay, but he loved football. For as long as Dusty could remember, he and Dad and Craig had played in the back yard. "But Craig always catches, and I always fumble," thought Dusty. He'd been thinking about that a lot.

As the whistle blew, Dusty turned back to the game. But his thoughts kept pace with the players on the field. Dad wanted him in sports. Dusty knew that soon Dad would start putting on more pressure.

"You guys need exercise," he often said. Craig had taken him at his word and gone out for football. But Dusty wasn't sure what to do.

"Craig's super-good," he thought. "I'm just not made like him."

As the second half started, Dusty leaned forward. Elbows on his knees, he rested his chin on his hands. "Wonder when I'll start getting hair on my face like

Craig," he thought, rubbing his cheeks. Then he felt his forehead. "More zits! Every time I turn around, there's a gob of 'em!"

Just then, Craig made a touchdown. Dusty jumped up and clapped and cheered with the rest. But his hurt was growing. "To everyone else Craig's the big hero. What's the use of trying to compete?"

When the game finished, 24-14, Central had won, but Dusty felt grumpy. Climbing down from the stands, he started off to meet Mom and Dad for the ride home. When he found them, they headed toward the car. But every few steps someone stopped them.

"Great son you got there!" called out one man. But Dusty knew he meant Craig.

Dad waved and said thanks, and kept on walking. But soon another man stopped him. "He'll get a football scholarship for sure, don't you think?"

Dusty walked on ahead. It was always this way. Craig this, Craig that. Craig, Craig, Craig. Dusty started to ache inside.

By the time he reached the car, he was quiet, but angry. When Dad said, "Let's go get some ice cream," Dusty answered, "Let's not, and say we did."

When Mom asked, "What's wrong, Dusty?" he told her, "Mind your own business." And, of course, Dad got after him for that.

For the next two days Dusty stormed around the house. One minute he wanted to act better. The next minute he didn't. And then he felt mad at himself. Finally he wheeled his bike out of the garage and took off on a long ride.

The wind felt good on his face. It wasn't long before he felt better. It was as though he could think again.

"I'll never be as good a football player as Craig," he thought. "So why do I keep telling myself I have to be?"

Before long, his thinking went a step further. "I don't wanna compete with him. What can I do instead?"

By the time Dusty had biked six blocks, he'd thought of several things. "Play golf? Too much money, unless I caddy. Tennis? Well, maybe. Jog? Cross-country ski?"

Then it hit him. Before now, it never seemed important. "I can swim!"

Slamming on his brakes, he spun his bike around. For the first time all week he felt excited.

The minute Dad got home from work, Dusty pounced on him. "Can we get a membership at the 'Y' so I can swim whenever I want?"

"Hmmmm," said Dad, looking surprised. Then he thought about it. "That might be a good choice. Swimming is something you can do the rest of your life. And your mom and I could use the membership, too."

When it was decided, Dusty started going to the "Y"

every day. At first he could swim only two lengths of the pool without stopping. But soon he decided it'd be fun to compete with himself. Each day he tried a little bit more. Every week his arms and shoulders grew stronger. Before long, he worked up to four lengths, and then six.

As he looked in the mirror one day, Dusty grinned at himself. His body was changing. And he had fewer zits. "Maybe all the exercise helps!"

When football season was over, Dusty's brother came to watch him do laps. "Way to go!" Craig called out.

Dusty felt warmed by his praise, but most of all, he felt good about himself.

TO TALK ABOUT

▶How did Dusty feel about his own body whenever he thought of Craig? How did Dusty compare his weaknesses with Craig's strengths?

▶How did Dusty think ahead? Why was his choice an especially good one for him? If his family couldn't afford a membership at the "Y," what other sports could Dusty have chosen?

▶What are some group sports in which the kids in your school take part? What are some good reasons for taking part in group sports?

▶Lifetime sports are ones in which a person can be

active without depending on a group. If people are healthy, they can participate in such sports for most of their lives. What are some of these sports? If you're active in group sports, why might it be good to also be active in a sport that doesn't depend on a group?

▶With many sports it's necessary to compete with other kids. How can it be helpful to pick a sport where you can just have fun, or compete only with yourself if you want?

▶How can improvement in a sport be a reward in itself? Why is it important for someone *not* in group sports to feel that reward?

▶How can taking care of your body by exercising be a way of honoring God?

God said, "So do not fear, for I am with you; do not be dismayed, for I am your God. I will strengthen you and help you; I will uphold you with my righteous right hand." (Isaiah 41:10)

Help me, Lord, to honor You by taking good care of my body. Help me to become active in sports that will give me the fun and exercise I need for a healthy body.

THROUGH
THE WALL

After school Mandy went over to Anna's house. The day before, Anna's mom had brought a new baby home from the hospital.

First Anna held her little sister, then her mother asked Mandy, "Do you want to hold the baby?"

Mandy felt scared. "What if I do something wrong?"

"I'll help you," she answered. "If you sit down in this big chair, I'll put her on your lap."

As Mandy held the baby, she forgot about being scared. "Wow! Look at all her blonde hair! And her cute little face!"

The baby's eyes were closed, and she slept peacefully. Mandy's arms tightened around her. It was the way she used to feel, holding her favorite doll. Only this one breathed and was real.

"Ever since Anna was born, we've wanted another child," said Anna's mom. "We waited a long time."

After a few minutes, the baby yawned, opened her eyes, and stretched her legs. Anna's mom pulled back the blanket so Mandy could see the baby's little feet. Then she helped Mandy uncurl the baby's fist. "Look at her fingernails!" Mandy exclaimed. "They're just like mine, but so *tiny!*"

To Mandy the baby was a miracle. She loved Anna's sister. "Can I come back and see her tomorrow?" she asked.

Soon after, Mandy needed to leave. When she reached home, it was time for supper. Mom set the serving dishes on the table, and everyone sat down.

Dad asked the blessing, but then silence hung heavy over the table. As she ate, Mandy watched Dad, then Mom, then her sixteen-year-old sister, Kay. Kay was pushing green beans around on her plate. Mom wasn't eating much either. But Dad was eating twice as much as usual. "What's wrong?" Mandy wanted to ask. She couldn't remember another meal when no one talked.

Mandy felt uncomfortable. "Are Mom and Dad mad?" she wondered. "Or do they feel bad about something?" Mandy wasn't sure.

Whatever it was, it was awful. And it had something to do with her sister. Kay sat there, just staring at her plate. Mom and Dad didn't even tell her to eat.

Finally Mandy broke the silence. "What's going on? What's the matter?"

"Mind your own business," Kay answered quickly.

Mom was silent, but her eyes pleaded, "Don't ask."

"It doesn't concern you," said Dad. Mandy knew he wouldn't say anything more.

The minute supper was over Kay went to her room. All evening Mandy felt uneasy being with Mom and Dad. Deep in their eyes, they looked hurt and sad and mad all at once. When Mandy went to bed, she still didn't know what was wrong.

She'd been sleeping for awhile when a sound woke her up. For a moment she lay still, trying to figure out what it was.

The sound came again. Then Mandy realized it was coming through the heat vent in the wall between her bedroom and Mom and Dad's.

As she listened, the words blurred together. Then Mandy heard Dad's voice, sharp and angry. "What's going on?" Mandy wondered for the hundredth time. "Dad hardly ever gets mad."

But then Kay's voice was even louder. "Don't yell at me!" she answered. "I said I'm sorry!"

Her voice softened. "I'm sorry I got myself into this. I'm sorry I'm pregnant."

"A baby?" thought Mandy. "Kay's gonna have a

133

baby? How can she have a baby when she isn't married?" Suddenly Mandy felt scared.

Kay's voice dropped, but Mandy could still hear. "I'm sorry I fooled around. I thought it would be fun."

Mom's voice was low, and Mandy couldn't pick out what she said. Then Kay spoke again. "You were right, Mom. You were right when you said it's important to wait to be married. I thought you were old-fashioned—that you didn't know what you were talking about. . . ."

Kay's voice broke off. Even through the wall, Mandy heard her sobs.

"I'm sorry I hurt you, Mom. I'm sorry, Dad." For a long moment there was silence, broken only by weeping. Then Kay spoke again. "I'll get an *abortion* so people don't find out. . . ."

"NO!" exclaimed Dad, and the word exploded. "You will *not* get an abortion!"

"An abortion?" Mandy almost said the word aloud. She'd heard about abortions on TV, but. . . .

Kay's voice had changed. "If I get an abortion, I won't have to have the baby. You won't have to be embarrassed. I know where I can go. I would've gone already if Mom hadn't caught on that I'm pregnant."

"An *abortion*?" Mom's voice sounded the way Mandy felt.

"Sure, Mom. It just takes a few minutes, and everything's all taken care of."

Just then Mandy remembered Anna's baby sister. The soft skin and blonde hair. The helpless little body. The tiny fingernails. The perfect toes.

"She'd kill a baby like that?" Mandy thought.

Deep inside Mandy, the tears started. She tried to push them away, but they kept coming. As she lay in bed, her shoulders began to shake. The tears spilled over and ran down her cheeks.

Mandy grabbed the blanket and pulled it up over her head, unable to listen anymore. "A little baby like Anna's sister? Kay would kill a baby like that?"

After a time, Mandy's sobs quieted, and she listened once again. Kay was speaking. "But if I have the baby, won't you be embarrassed?"

"That's not what's important," said Mom. "What you did is wrong. But we'll stick by you because we love you."

Kay started crying again. As Mandy listened, she wondered if Kay would be happy again.

For a long time Mandy lay awake, thinking about Anna's baby sister.

TO TALK ABOUT

▶When Anna's mother had a baby, it was a special time in their house. When Kay talked about being pregnant, it was awful. What made the difference?

▶When people sin, they often say, "God could never

forgive me for what I've done." Yet if Kay asks God, He *will* forgive her. What words could Kay use to ask God's forgiveness?

▶ *Whatever* the sin is, God forgives *everyone* who is truly sorry and asks forgiveness. At the same time, people often have to live with the results of their sin. For Kay that might mean her choices are limited. What are some things she might not be able to do with her life?

▶ What are some choices Kay will need to make about the baby?

▶ If Kay has an abortion, what will happen to the baby? How do you feel about that? How do you think God feels about abortions?

▶ Who is the Giver of life? Why is every life valuable to Him?

You saw me before I was born and scheduled each day of my life when I began to breathe. Every day was recorded in Your Book! (Psalm 139:16, TLB)

Thank You, God, that every life is created by You. Help me remember how much You value every life. Help me to keep the creation of new life as something holy and beautiful.

KARA WAITS

On that Friday morning in July, Kara was sitting in the kitchen, putting on nail polish. When the phone rang, she thought, "It won't be for me," and kept on with her nails.

But the phone kept ringing, and her older sister, Sabrina, called out, "Will you get it, Kara? I'm in the tub."

Kara sighed and took her time about getting to the phone. "Hello?" she said. She was right, of course. It was for Sabrina.

The minute Sabrina knew it was Danny, she was out of the tub, into a bathrobe, and at the phone. "Tonight? Right. That'll be fun. See you at 6:30."

As she hung up, Sabrina glowed. "Wow! Do you

know *what?* Do you know who *that* was?"

"Yep, I know," answered Kara, not feeling very excited. As far as she was concerned, it was just one more boy on Sabrina's list.

"He's only the coolest guy in the whole school! And he asked me out!"

Kara tried to pretend she cared, but her smile felt stiff. She was glad when her sister left to get dressed. "Always Sabrina," she thought. "Always, always, always. Sure, Mom says I'm too young to date. But even when I'm old enough, who'll ask me out? What if I *never* get any dates?"

Once more Kara sighed, just thinking about the way Sabrina looked. As she glanced up, she saw two pictures on a shelf above the sink. Sabrina—slender and lovely, long dark hair blowing in the wind. "And then there's me," thought Kara. "Long, skinny legs. Mousey hair. Chest like a boy." As she bent her head to finish her nails, Kara blinked away tears.

Then she remembered the slumber party that night. "Well, at least I can go to Abby's." Kara always had fun when she stayed there.

Just then the phone rang, and she picked it up again.

"Hi, Kara," said a warm voice on the other end of the line.

"Hey, Aunt Mickey!" Something in Kara jumped, just hearing the sound of her voice. Mickey was Mom's younger sister who had never married. She was a social worker and lived almost 200 miles away.

"Riiiiight!" answered Mickey. "Just found out I need to come your way to pick up a runaway girl. How about if I stay overnight? Then we can talk before I have to leave in the morning. How does that sound?"

"Sabrina has a date, and Mom isn't here," answered Kara. "But I'm sure it'll be okay with her."

Yet as she answered, Kara felt uneasy. "Will it *really* be okay with Mom?" she wondered. After Dad left them, Mom started dating. Often she had even more dates than Sabrina.

But Kara pushed her uneasiness aside. "It'll be great to have you come!" she said to Mickey. "We haven't seen you for a long time."

"I know. I'm lonesome for you. I'm not sure exactly when I'll be there, but probably around seven, okay?"

"Okaaaay! Great!"

As Kara got off the phone, she felt warm clear through, just thinking about Mickey. Her aunt's name was really Michelle, but back when Kara was little, she started calling her Mickey. The name had stuck, just like the special relationship between them.

But Sabrina wasn't happy to hear about Mickey coming. "I have a date, you know."

"I know. I told her. You don't have to be here," answered Kara. Then she remembered. "Oh, wow! I've got that slumber party at Abby's tonight. Oh well,

Mom can take care of Mickey."

But when Mom got home from work, she said, "I can't be here. I've got a dinner date."

"Aw, Mommmmmm," answered Kara. "You're always going out. Can't you change it to another night?"

Mom shook her head. "Nope. You told her she could come. You take care of her. I've only got an hour to get ready."

"But I'm supposed to go to Abby's!" Kara wailed. "Can't Mickey go out to eat with you?"

Kara wasn't surprised that Mom didn't like that idea. "Let's just leave a key for her," Mom said. "Mickey can come in and go to bed early. She won't mind."

Soon Sabrina and Mom left, and Kara got ready for Abby's. She had everything in her backpack when she wondered how Aunt Mickey would feel, coming into an empty house. "It'll be worse than when I'm all alone. Mickey doesn't know anyone around here."

Since Dad left, Kara had been alone a lot. She thought about it. "Even though I'd rather be at Abby's, it's not fair. Mickey's nice."

Inside, she felt torn, wanting to treat her aunt the way Mickey always treated her. Yet, even more, Kara wanted to be at the slumber party. "Here I am, home alone again. Everyone but me having a date."

Then Kara remembered how Aunt Mickey always managed to laugh about something. Kara tried to laugh, but it didn't work. Taking her backpack to her room, she dropped it in a corner. Then she called Abby and said she wasn't coming.

After an hour of waiting, Kara wondered if it was worth it. "Maybe Mickey won't show up." Finally she went to her room for the backpack. As soon as she picked it up, Kara dropped it again. "Mickey's never broken a promise." That was one of the things Kara liked about her.

Just then a car door slammed. Kara hurried to the front window. Sure enough, it was Mickey!

Running down the walk, Kara threw herself into Mickey's arms.

"Hey, hey, hey! Good to see you!" Mickey held Kara back, taking a long look. "Wow! What a lovely woman you've become!"

"Me?" asked Kara, wanting to believe her, but afraid to hope.

"Yep," said Mickey, a smile spreading across her face. "*You!* Just the way you look! I like your hair that way. And you still give a super hug!"

"Thanks," said Kara gratefully. Mickey hadn't changed. She still had the same dark hair Mom used to have. And Mickey's eyes were warm and caring. Kara knew Mickey was a Christian and wondered if that's what made her so nice.

Kara helped Mickey bring her bag into the house. As she looked around, Mickey asked, "Your mom and Sabrina are gone? They both have a date?"

"Yeah," answered Kara. "Sorry about that." She felt embarrassed that her mom and Sabrina hadn't tried to change their plans, since Mickey came so seldom.

"Well, then, let's celebrate that you and I are together," said Mickey. "Let's go out to eat somewhere. Somewhere really nice, okay?"

"Okay!" answered Kara.

In a few minutes they were off. For the first time since she'd seen Mickey a year ago, Kara talked without stopping. There was something about her aunt that made Kara feel she could tell her anything.

They went to a country inn, and it was fun to be in such a nice place. It was even more fun to talk, just the two of them. But when they were having dessert, Mickey asked, "Kara, how are you *really* doin'?"

Kara blinked, trying to hold back the tears, but they came anyway. Mickey waited until Kara could speak. It took three tries before she made it. "Mickey, do you ever feel like you're a zero?"

Mickey laughed, and Kara felt sorry she'd asked. But when Mickey answered, her voice was soft. "Lots of times. Lots and lots of times. You see, I have a good-looking older sister. . . ."

In spite of herself Kara grinned.

"And lots of times I thought I'd *never* be asked out."

"You really thought that?"

"I really thought that."

"But you were . . . I mean, you *have* been. . . ." Kara stopped, not wanting to hurt her aunt.

"Not much in high school," said Mickey. "Boys always asked your mom. But later on, yes—when they started looking for a wife."

She winked. "I'm good wife material, they think."

"But you didn't get married."

"Nope, I didn't, and I don't feel sorry. Some people feel sorry for me, I'm sure, but that's their problem. It's not mine."

"How come? I mean, how come you haven't gotten married?"

"Because I never felt God had connected me with the right man," said Mickey. "It's much better not to marry than to marry the wrong person."

"But do you ever feel like . . . like you're . . .?" Kara stopped.

"Like I'm not worth anything? Like I'm not sexy, or . . .?" Mickey grinned, but her eyes were serious. "You know, Kara, dating's fun, especially if it's with the right person. But it isn't *all* there is in life. And sometimes girls do wrong things because they think they'll get more dates that way. It never works—not in the long run."

Mickey set down her iced tea. "Kara, I don't want to spend my whole life looking for a man. If God puts one in my path, that's great. But if He doesn't, that's okay. It's okay to *not* get married.

"I have a full life," Mickey went on. "I'm growing in new ways all the time. Because I'm not tied down with a family, there're a lot of things I can do—ways I can help other people. But you see, if I'm married or not married, it has nothing to do with my sexuality. I'm still a whole person."

"Do you ever get. . . ?" Kara stopped again.

"Ever get lonely? Yep, sometimes," answered Mickey. "Times like that I try to reach out to others— to see if there's a way I can help them. Times like that I come and see you."

Kara grinned. "And take me out for supper."

"I'm taking *you*? Oooops!" Mickey laughed. "Better see if I have enough money."

In that moment, Kara felt glad she'd skipped the slumber party. But it wasn't until they returned home that Mickey discovered what had happened. When she went into Kara's bedroom, she saw the backpack in the corner and asked, "Going somewhere?"

Kara had never lied to Mickey, and she didn't want to start. But when she answered Mickey's question, she wasn't prepared for the tears that came to her aunt's eyes.

"Kara, I'm glad that you were here when I came," she said.

Kara smiled. "Me, too."

"I'm glad to know you're still the kind of person

you are," Mickey went on. "Keep on being that way, okay?"

Kara nodded. "I'll try."

"But it's getting late, and I've got a long drive tomorrow. I really need to go to bed. Couldn't you still go to the slumber party? You'll stay up all night talking, won't you?"

Again Kara nodded, her thoughts already jumping ahead to the fun she could have.

"I'll drive you there, okay?" Mickey asked.

This time it was Kara's turn to feel tears in her eyes. "Wow! I get to do both things!" she thought. She hugged her aunt so tight that Mickey squealed.

TO TALK ABOUT

▶What were some of the things that bothered Kara about her sister, Sabrina? What were some things about her mom that bothered Kara?

▶What kind of person do you think Mickey was? How can you tell from the story?

▶Mickey chose not to marry, and said, "I'm a whole person." What does it mean to be a whole person? How did Mickey feel about her life?

▶Every one of us needs to know it's okay to be what we are. In what ways did Mickey give Kara that message?

▶What did you like about Kara and Mickey's relationship? How did they help each other? What miracle do you think Kara experienced in the way she felt about herself?

▶ Kara wanted to go to the slumber party, yet she wanted to be at home with Mickey. Have you ever been torn between feeling you should do something and wanting to do something else? What happened?

▶ Kara longed to date, but she learned a secret of the heart instead. What was that secret?

▶ What are some good things about being single? Have you thought about the fact that both Jesus and the Apostle Paul were single? Does being single mean you have to be lonely? Why or why not? Do you think some married people are lonely?

▶ Aunt Mickey had accepted the way she was. She helped Kara accept the way Kara was. Is there some way in which you need to say, "It's okay to be the way I am"? Explain what you mean.

"The King [Jesus] will reply, 'I tell you the truth, whatever you did for one of the least of these brothers of mine, you did for me.'" (Matthew 25:40)

Jesus, a lot of times I feel I'm not terrific like somebody else. I keep feeling sorry for myself. Help me to accept myself the way I am. Then help me to think about the feelings of others.

A NOTE FOR AARON

When the note came to Aaron's desk, a tingle of dread went through him. This had happened before—right after Dad became manager of the town bowling alley. Folded small, wrinkled and dirty, the note looked like it'd passed through many hands. Yet clearly it had Aaron's name on it.

Glancing up, he saw kids turn in his direction. "They'll watch me 'til I open it," he thought.

A minute later the teacher left the room, and Aaron unfolded the note. It was for him, all right. "To Aaron," it began. Then, as he saw the words, he felt himself turn red all over.

On one side was a cartoon—how he looked when walking across the school stage at the fall concert.

Because teachers knew Aaron was gifted, he'd played a piano solo between the band and choir numbers.

The note described Aaron's toothpick legs: "You look like a skinny girl. You're dumb, and you're a sissy. Only girls play the piano. You don't have a friend in the whole world."

Worst of all were the kind of words used. Aaron wasn't sure what some of the words meant. But the few he did know told him too much. From the top of his head down to his toes, he felt dirty. "Wish I could crawl in a hole," he thought.

He wanted to shout, "I hate you!" Just in time, he remembered that whoever wrote the note was probably watching. Slipping it into his jeans pocket, Aaron tried not to show how he felt. Just the same, the words burned into his mind.

In the next two days he acted as if nothing had happened. Yet now and then, when he was by himself, he took out the note and re-read it. The third time through, he saw it had four or five different kinds of handwriting. "Did they pass it around?" he wondered. "It looks like each kid added something."

From then on, whenever Aaron looked at someone in his classroom, he wondered, "Are you one of them? Did you write that note?"

The more Aaron thought about the words in the note, the more he dreaded going back to school each day. Most of all, he dreaded playing the piano at the spring concert. It was only a week away.

A month before, he'd finished memorizing his song, *Prelude in C Sharp Minor* by Rachmaninoff [Rahk-MAHN-ih-nawf]. But suddenly, as he practiced one evening, Aaron couldn't remember the music. His mind went blank except for two thoughts: "They think I look like a girl. They think I'm a sissy."

Then Aaron remembered the rest of the note. "I'm dumb just like they said. I don't have a friend in the world. How can I play in front of the whole school?"

In that moment everything seemed impossible. Aaron's hands crashed down on the piano. For a long time he sat there, holding his head in his hands.

His dad found Aaron there. "Hey, what's the matter?"

"Nothing," Aaron answered, unwilling to look at Dad's face.

Just then Mom joined them. "That's not true. I can tell by the way you're playing. What's wrong?"

Aaron stared at the piano keys without answering. Finally, feeling as if he were moving in slow motion, he dug into his jeans pocket. Without a word, he handed the note to Dad.

"I see," said Dad, after reading the note. He handed it to Mom.

As Mom read, her face crumpled. "Oh, Aaron, that's awful. How long have you had this?"

"Since Monday."

Mom blinked away the tears on her lashes. "How did it make you feel?"

For a long moment Aaron couldn't speak. When he did, his voice was low. "Maybe they're right. Maybe I *am* dumb. I sure do have toothpick legs. Am I a sissy because I play the piano?"

Suddenly his voice was angry. "Why me? What did I do to make all the kids pick on me?"

Once again Dad looked at the note. "Maybe it's not you they're picking on. Last weekend I had to ask five or six kids your age to stop hanging around the bowling alley. When one of them swore at me, I told him to stop talking that way."

Dad looked thoughtful. "If that's what happened, I'm sorry they took it out on you. *Really* sorry. I was right in what I did, but I'm sorry for you."

"I was afraid to tell you."

"Hey, you can always talk to us," said Dad. "We're all in this together. We love you, remember?"

Slowly Aaron nodded. "Do you think I'll get more dirty notes after this concert? I keep thinking about that, and I'm scared."

As Mom and Dad talked, Aaron had an idea. "Most of the great piano players have been men. I wonder if they all got picked on?"

A new thought dropped into his mind. "I'll never be able to please everyone. Just because kids say something about me doesn't mean that's what I am."

Turning to the piano, Aaron started the *Prelude* again. But as soon as he thought about the kids, his fingers felt clumsy. When he missed one note after another, he stopped.

"It's only a week away! How can I play in the concert?" Aaron's voice rose. "How can I play in front of those kids?"

When Dad spoke, his voice was quiet and gentle. "When someone really hurts you, there's only one thing to do."

"What's that?"

"Forgive them," answered Dad.

"But how?" Aaron's voice was angry. "The note's so awful. I wanna hate those kids! If I forgive 'em, I'll be saying that what they did was okay!"

"Not on your life!" answered Dad. "You're forgiving them because Jesus told us to do that. And as a result, you'll start feeling better."

Aaron wasn't sure he believed Dad. For a long moment he thought about it. Then he thought about the concert and how his fingers wouldn't move. "I don't have any choice, do I?"

"Nope," said Dad.

Aaron said a quick prayer in his mind. "Jesus, I forgive those kids." He wondered if he really meant what he'd prayed. "Maybe sometime I'll *feel* it," he thought.

Then he thought about all the times he'd read

that note. Taking it from Mom, Aaron tore the note into tiny bits, and tossed them in a wastebasket. He was surprised what a relief that was.

Yet when the day of the concert arrived, Aaron felt like hot oil skittering on a frying pan. Each time he saw the kids, his hurt started to come back.

But then he remembered tearing up the note. "I've forgiven 'em," he thought. "I don't want to think about it again!"

In that moment something changed inside Aaron. To his surprise he didn't hate the kids anymore. Instead, a plan formed in his mind. He knew exactly what he'd do.

That night, when it was time for Aaron's solo, he felt more scared than he'd ever been. More than anything, he didn't want those kids to know how nervous he felt.

Crossing the stage, he sat down on the piano bench and turned to the audience. At first it seemed a blur, a wilderness of faces. Then he saw Mom and Dad.

His lips felt stiff, but Aaron smiled. Mom smiled back, and Dad looked like he wanted to clap.

Then Aaron turned back to the piano. "Jesus," he thought. The name was a prayer. He felt a sureness flow through him. As he held his hands above the keyboard, they steadied.

Aaron struck the opening octaves of *Prelude in C Sharp Minor.* As his fingers sank into the chords, the auditorium grew still. Aaron forgot about the kids who listened. He forgot about the words they'd written. He just felt the music. Its fire raced through his fingers. Every note fell clean and sure.

When the applause broke around him, Aaron stood and took his bows. Once again he smiled. This time his smile was real.

TO TALK ABOUT

▶When the kids made fun of how Aaron looked, how did it make him feel about his body? About his ability to play the piano?

▶The kids may have sent Aaron the note because of what happened at the bowling alley, or they may have had another reason. Do you think any of them felt jealous of Aaron? Why or why not?

▶What are the steps Aaron took to work out his problem?

▶Why is it important that he talked with his mom and dad about the note?

▶If Aaron hadn't torn up the note, his feelings about it probably would have gotten even worse. Why?

▶Has anyone ever said something mean about your physical appearance? How did it make you feel? What did you do about it?

▶The story says that the dirty words burned into Aaron's mind. If you've had mean words, dirty or

155

otherwise, said about you, you know it's hard to forget them. The best way is to forgive the person who hurt you. Next ask Jesus to clean those thoughts out of your mind. Then if the words come back, remember His promise to forgive you. Keep thinking about Jesus.

Jesus said, "Happy are you when people insult you and persecute you and tell all kinds of evil lies against you because you are my followers. Be happy and glad, for a great reward is kept for you in heaven." (Matthew 5:11-12, GNB)

Jesus, it really hurts when someone's mean to me. Yet I know that when people treated You that way, You forgave them. Because of that, Jesus, I forgive the kids who've hurt me. Heal me, so their words don't hurt me anymore.

AT HOME NEXT DOOR

Quietly Darcy shut the back door behind her. "Wow! It feels good to shut out the sound of Mom and Dad fighting!"

Without making a sound, she slipped down the steps, then through the yard to the neighbor's house. A moment later she knocked on their back door.

To Darcy's relief, Nita answered the door. Nita was seventeen, and five years older than Darcy. "Hi, come on in," she said. "Haven't seen you for awhile."

Darcy said hi, then felt shy. Nita made her feel welcome. "I've missed you. Remember how we used to talk about things?"

Darcy nodded, feeling miserable inside. Now that she was here, she didn't know what to say.

But Nita filled in the gaps. "I just made some cookies. Why don't you have some with me?" Soon Darcy was sitting at the kitchen table, and before she knew it, it was like old times. Even when Darcy was a little girl, Nita had been like a big sister to her. When it got too hard at home, Darcy came here.

Nita knew that. "What's the matter?" she asked after the third cookie.

"I just . . . just. . . ." Darcy stopped as the tears began spilling down her cheeks.

"Are your mom and dad fighting again?" asked Nita.

Slowly Darcy nodded.

"How're you feeling about it?"

Darcy thought for a moment. "I'm not scared the way I was when I was a little kid. Then I always wondered if they'd hurt me. Beat me up, I mean. They never have, but. . . ."

Darcy stopped, trying to think it through. "Now I get scared in other ways. Boys at school notice me, and sometimes I like them. . . ."

Nita waited, so Darcy had to go on.

"But what if. . . ?"

Again Darcy stopped. Still Nita waited.

"What if they treat me. . . ?"

This time Nita helped her out. "The way your dad treats your mom? That's a good question."

"When I see your mom and dad. . . . They have a

good time together. They act like they *love* each other."

"Yeah, they do," said Nita. "Every now and then they disagree about something, but they talk it out. They *do* love each other."

"And when I come over here. . . ."

Nita helped her finish. "It's different, isn't it?"

Darcy nodded, and looked down at the kitchen floor. She was afraid to tell Nita how miserable she really felt.

But Nita guessed. "Darcy, are you wondering about this because when you grow up, you want to be happy like my mom and dad?"

"Sounds kind of dumb, huh? Thinking about it now?"

"Sounds kind of smart to me."

"For you it's easy," said Darcy. "You can watch your mom and dad. You can try to be like them. But what about me?"

"That's true," Nita answered. "It *is* easier for me. But you can learn from my mom and dad, too. Pick out what you like about the way they live. They aren't perfect, any more than anyone else. But try to remember what you like."

"But. . . ." Darcy didn't know how to say it, but she tried, "Why do your mom and dad have it so good, and my mom and dad have it so awful?"

Nita thought for a moment. "Well, the most

important thing is that they're both Christians. That doesn't always mean a marriage is going to be good, but it helps. Mom and Dad pray together, and when they disagree about something they ask Jesus to help them with it."

"How did they get together?"

Nita grinned. "When I was a little kid I thought this sounded stupid. But now that I see some of the boys out there, I don't anymore. When my mom was still a young girl, her mom—my grandma—taught her to pray about who she'd marry. And the funny part about it is that my dad's dad—my grandpa—taught *him* to pray about who *he'd* marry!"

"How did they know what to look for?"

Again Nita grinned. "Well, I can tell you *that.* Or at least I'll tell you what *I'm* looking for!"

"You think I'm dumb asking now?" Darcy asked again.

"NO! It's important to know *before* you start dating. For both boys and girls, it's important. Well, let's see. First of all, I want a Christian—and one who feels as strongly about being a Christian as I do. Some girls marry guys that go to church, but they really aren't as strongly committed, and they wind up having a problem."

For a moment Nita was quiet. "And I want someone who respects me."

"What does that mean?"

"Well, when you go out on a date, some boys want to see what they can get away with. They want to take you to a lonely place and park. So don't let yourself get stuck in a lonely place. Or don't invite a boy over when your mom and dad are working. Sometimes girls think, 'I'll lose my boyfriend if I don't do what he wants.' Instead, that's the surest way to lose him."

"So it's okay to say no?" asked Darcy.

"You bet it's okay to say no! That's being good to yourself. And it's okay to say, 'I don't want to be pushed.' It's okay to have ideals."

"Ideals?"

"To wait with sex until marriage," answered Nita. "A speaker came to school, and he said studies show that people who wait have a better chance of being happy within marriage."

"But what if a boy really loves me?"

"Oh, lots of boys will say they love you. And they'll say to you, 'If you love me, prove it.'"

"Prove it?"

"Yeah, that's the line they use to get girls to go farther sexually than the girls want to go," said Nita. "That's where a lot of girls get stuck with someone who's wrong for them."

"But you're sure someone like that wouldn't really love me?"

"Not on your life. If someone really loves you, he cares about what happens to you. He wouldn't purposely do something that would hurt you."

Nita leaned forward. "You want to do things you really want to do—like graduate from high school and work or go to college. You want to wait for a husband you *really* love. If a guy doesn't respect you, he can make *you* lose respect for yourself. And self-respect is one of the most important things you have."

For a moment Nita was quiet. "And there's something more."

"What's that?" asked Darcy.

"Saying no to sex outside of marriage is one way of acting the way God wants you to act. It's dreaming big. It's letting God help you become all He wants you to be."

For a moment the kitchen was quiet. Then Darcy thought of another question. "How will I know if I really love someone?"

"It'll be someone you think a lot of," said Nita, counting off her ideas on her fingers. "You respect him, and the way he acts. You can talk with him—even about hard things. You have fun together. And you don't have to spend a lot of money to do it. Oh, and you like doing nice things for him."

"And he's good-lookin'. . . ."

Nita grinned. "Of course!" Then her eyes turned serious. "But my mom says when you love someone, no matter how that person looks, he seems good-looking."

"What about love at first sight?"

Nita laughed. "Wow! I can tell you've really been thinking about this. Well, from what my mom says. . . ."

A voice interrupted. "And what does your mom say?"

Darcy looked up, glad to see Nita's mom, but wishing she hadn't come now.

"My mom-m-m says," Nita drawled, "there's a difference between being attracted to a boy and really loving him. You can like the way a boy looks at first sight. But love. . . ."

Nita and her mom said it together. "Love grows."

"You need to give it time so you know for sure," said Nita's mom.

Darcy stood up. "Gotta go now. Thanks for the cookies."

Nita went to the door with her and gave Darcy a hug. "Come over again—soon, okay?"

Darcy nodded, knowing she'd be back. "Thanks, Nita," she said softly. Then she bounded across the yard and slipped through the back door. As she tiptoed up the stairs to her room, the house was quiet. Mom and Dad had stopped fighting—until the next time.

As Darcy crawled into bed, she prayed for them. Then, for the first time, she prayed about who she might someday marry.

TO TALK ABOUT

▶Why is it helpful to spend a lot of time with groups of kids before you start dating one person?

▶When you start to date, what are some of the qualities you want to look for in the persons you date?

▶Why is it important to know how you want to handle yourself on a date? Why is it important to know that *before* you start dating?

▶Every boy needs to be responsible in the way he acts. Being responsible means respecting a girl and being thoughtful about what's best for her. What are some ways a boy can be responsible toward a girl?

▶How can a girl be responsible in the way she treats a boy?

▶Galatians 5:22-25 says something important about self-control. What is self-control?

▶Often teenagers believe they're in love and later discover it was an infatuation, a liking for someone that doesn't last. How would you feel if you got too serious with a boy or girl, then discovered you didn't "love" them anymore?

▶The Bible tells us that sexual intercourse outside marriage is a sin against our bodies. Yet within marriage, intercourse is beautiful and God's way for a man and woman to express love to one another. How can the way a person acts sexually be a matter of obedience to God? (Obedience is responding to what

God likes, not because we have to, but because we love Him.)

▶See 1 Corinthians 6:18-20. What does it mean to be a temple of the Holy Spirit? What does it mean to honor God with your body?

▶Dating can be exciting and fun, or it can be a time of misery. What do you think makes the difference?

▶What are some ways to know if love is real? Some clues are in the story. You'll find more ideas in 1 Corinthians 13.

▶Whether you're a boy or girl, why is it important to pray about who you might marry?

Do you not know that your body is a temple of the Holy Spirit, who is in you, whom you have received from God? You are not your own; you were bought at a price. Therefore honor God with your body.
(1 Corinthians 6:19-20)

Thank You, Jesus, that right now I can learn a lot about others by having fun with groups of kids. Help me know what qualities to look for in whoever I date. If You want me to get married someday, I want to marry the person You know is right for me.

165

THE DAY OF THE STORM

As Pete sat at the supper table, he stretched out his leg. Suddenly he kicked his twin sister, Pam.

"Stop it!" she exclaimed, glaring at Pete.

Pete's leg was already back under his chair. He looked as innocent as a newborn baby.

Mom sighed. "What's the matter with you two? All day long—fight, fight, fight."

Dad put down his fork and looked up. "Leave your sister alone, Pete. As long as you're done, you can start the dishes."

"Dishes? That's girl's work!"

"Girl's work?" asked Dad.

"Yeah, girl's work! You don't really expect me

to do the dishes, do you?"

"Yes, I do," answered Dad.

"But only girls do dishes. That's Pam's job."

"You just don't wanna do 'em," said Pam.

Mom looked at Pam, then at Pete. "I think she's right, Pete."

Groaning, he stood up. With every dish he carried to the sink, he had a new complaint. Finally Dad said, "No more comments, Pete, okay?"

"Yeah, Peteeerrrr!" drawled Pam.

Mom looked at Dad and rolled her eyes. Clearly she was tired of their arguing.

Dad looked thoughtful. "Pam, I'd like to have you mow the lawn."

"Da-d-d-d-d! You've gotta be kidding. *Me* mow the lawn?"

"Yes, *you* mow the lawn," answered Dad. "It's supposed to rain tonight, so I think you should get started right away."

"But what if someone sees me? I'd be so embarrassed doing Pete's work!"

Dad grinned. "Oh? Pete's work? You're sure?"

"I'm sure! I don't wanna get all hot and sweaty!"

"Hey, I'll trade with you, Pam," Pete said quickly.

Dad winked at Mom. "Nope, no trades," he said. "Not tonight. I think we should do a bit of thinking about male and female roles around here."

"Oh, Da-d-d-d-d!" they groaned. This time Pam

and Pete complained in unison.

"I mean it! Is there such a thing as boy's work and girl's work? Or can we all just pitch in when something needs to be done?"

Mom smiled, but neither Pam nor Pete seemed to like Dad's idea. He went on. "I haven't thought much about it before, but maybe your mom and I have taught you to fill certain roles just by the way we treat you. Is that good or bad or somewhere in between?"

Pete jumped on it. "That's good! Look at the name you gave me. I'm a rock!" He flexed the muscles in his arms. "Strength, power, everything you want!"

Just then he had an idea. As he picked up another plate, he let his voice sound only half-interested. "What does Pam's name mean anyway?"

"Loving, kind," answered Mom, falling into the trap. "All honey."

"All honey!" Pete hooted. "She's all honey, all right!"

Pam's eyes glistened with anger. "I don't know why I have to have you for a brother!"

Dad's grin faded. "Okay, that's enough. Both of you get to work." He stood up. "It's getting dark, Pam. Get the mowing done right away." Dad picked up his paper and went into the living room.

As Pete washed the dishes, he looked out the kitchen window. Only fifteen minutes had passed, but dark clouds hurried across the sky. Already they'd moved directly overhead.

Pam had the lawn only half mowed when the wind came up, whipping through the trees.

Pete left the dishes and headed for the back yard. "Hey, Pam! Go for it!" Grabbing the handle, he pushed the mower as fast as he could toward the garage. Slamming the door shut, he followed her to the house.

Just as he reached the kitchen door, the wind pushed him against the house. A strong gust roared through a nearby maple, and Pete heard a crack. A large limb landed on the lawn.

Dad met him at the door. "Head for the basement!"

With a bound Pete reached the steps, and took them two at a time. Partway down, he twisted his ankle and tumbled the rest of the way.

As he landed at the bottom of the steps, Pete groaned. Clutching his ankle, he rolled on the floor. "Ow, ow, ow!"

As he looked up, Mom and Dad and Pam knelt around him, their eyes full of concern.

"Did you hit your head?" asked Mom.

"Oh, Pete, I'm sorry," said Pam. "It's 'cause you were helping me."

"It's 'cause I was doing girl's work," Pete said, his voice angry. "If I'd been mowing the lawn, I'd have been done!"

As he tried to sit up, he moved his leg and winced. "Owwwww!" Lying back down again, Pete groaned.

"Just take it easy," said Dad. "Lie still for a minute."

"Did you feel anything snap?" asked Mom.

Pete shook his head.

"Can you move your foot?" Dad asked.

As Pete tried to move his leg, he winced. The pain brought tears to his eyes.

"Boys aren't supposed to cry," said Pam sweetly, sounding like her old self.

Suddenly Dad and Mom laughed.

"I don't see what's funny," Pete grumbled. "I'm lying here dying, and you're all laughing."

Just then the lights flickered and went out. In the darkness Pete heard Mom laugh again, but this time there was another sound in her laughter. She was close to tears.

"Take it easy, honey," said Dad. "Where's the flashlight that's supposed to be down here?"

"It's on the shelf," said Pam. "Just a sec. I'll get it." In a minute she had it in her hand. Soon she'd also found and lit the candles they kept in the basement.

A moment later she turned on the battery operated radio. "Straight-line winds have left a path of destruction through the center part of the state. . . ."

Mom was still on the floor next to Pete. "I think it's a sprain, but we'd better make sure."

"The brunt of the storm has now left the metro area," the newscaster went on. "Cleanup crews will be

171

out shortly, clearing the main roads."

Carefully Dad slid a pillow under Pete's leg. "Let's give it another fifteen minutes. Then we better take you in to emergency."

When it was time to go to the hospital, Mom and Dad helped Pete up the steps and into the car. As soon as Pam jumped in, Dad backed out of the driveway. He drove slowly, weaving around the branches in the road. "Good thing it's only six blocks."

But for Pete it seemed like sixty miles. Glumly he stared out the window and tried not to move his leg. It seemed to be hurting more every minute.

Already, crews were out with chainsaws, trying to clear away the fallen branches. An electric company van blocked one street as three people worked on a power line.

"See! A woman's working with 'em!" said Pam, turning to Pete.

"Hush!" said Mom. "Leave him alone!"

Dad turned around, but two blocks away they ran into trouble again. The signal lights were out, but someone in a yellow raincoat waved them through the intersection. Pete didn't need Pam's help to see that the police officer was a woman.

Pam stayed in the waiting room, and Mom and Dad helped Pete into the emergency room. Before long, a man dressed in a white shirt and pants appeared beside Pete's bed. As he started asking questions, Pete had a question for him. "Are you the doctor?"

"Nope, I'm a nurse," the man answered. "Let's see what you've got here." Gently he pulled down Pete's sock. "Now, this is going to be a bit uncomfortable, but I need to get your sock and shoe off before it swells any more."

An hour later Pete left the hospital, Mom on one side, Dad on the other. Pam trailed behind again. It was a bad sprain. The doctor said Pete would have to use crutches and stay off his ankle for awhile.

In the time that followed, Pete took full advantage of the doctor's orders. Whenever he could, he ordered Pam around. But often he thought about all that had happened the day of the storm. He started to watch Dad to see how he handled certain things.

"Here, let me get that," said Dad one day, when Mom had a heavy grocery bag in the car.

Another time Dad said, "Praying's not a sign of weakness." After that, Pete noticed how often Dad prayed, when it seemed he was just sitting in his chair.

But one night when Mom was really tired, Pete caught Dad doing the dishes. Once Pete would have said, "That's sissy stuff!" Instead, he asked Dad, "You're helping Mom, aren't you?" It wasn't really a question. Pete knew the answer.

Dad smiled. "When you were a baby, your mom worked extra long hours because I couldn't get a job. I changed your diapers. I did the dishes. I'm not a sissy. I just respect your mother and want to help her."

As Dad let the water out of the sink, he winked. "And sometimes, in the middle of winter, she helps me shovel the snow."

Lying in bed that night Pete thought about it. "I'm glad I'm a boy," he told himself. "I *like* being what I am."

But he never asked Pam how she felt about being a girl. Pete thought he knew what she'd say.

TO TALK ABOUT

▶ Pete said that doing dishes was girl's work. What do you think he was really saying?

▶ Pam said, "Boys aren't supposed to cry." What do you think she was really saying? Can you remember a time when Jesus cried? (See John 11:35.) Why is it important that both boys and girls feel free to cry when they need to?

▶ As a man and a woman, Pete's dad and mom had God-given differences. Yet that didn't divide them. Instead, the differences in the way they were made helped them work together. They seemed happy in their male and female roles. What qualities made Pete's dad a special person? What qualities made Pete's mom a special person?

▶ Male and female roles have changed. The kind of

work you do is not as important as whether you're willing to help someone and work together. When you care about others, you want the best for them, the way Jesus does. What happened as long as Pete made himself number one? Was he happy? Why or why not?

▶What happened as long as Pam bugged Pete? Do you think she was happy? Why or why not?

▶A role model is someone who helps you know what kind of person you want to be. That person acts in a way you'd like to act, or does things you'd like to do. If you're a girl, why is it important that you *like* being a girl? What women in the Bible would you like to be like?

▶If you're a boy, why is it important that you *like* being a boy? What men in the Bible would you like to be like?

▶Whether you're a boy or a girl, who is the very best role model you can have? Why?

Love is very patient and kind, never jealous or envious, never boastful or proud, never haughty or selfish or rude. Love does not demand its own way.
(1 Corinthians 13:4-5, TLB)

I like being what I am, Lord. Thank You that I'm living at a time when I'm free to try many different kinds of work. Help me to value the good things about being a male and the good things about being a female.

YOU ARE WONDERFULLY MADE!

While reading this book, you met a number of new kids. You learned about their choices. Perhaps you've already made choices of your own. As times goes on, you'll be making more of them.

Maybe you also discovered that many small choices add up to big ones. That's how you choose the side you want to be on—the side that values your body as something special.

That's also God's side. He values you. He values you exactly the way you are. But when you think about choosing His side, you may tell yourself, "I want to make good choices, but I don't know if I can."

When you feel that way, you're in a great spot. In

177

those times you can ask, "God, what do You want me to do? How do You want me to live?" You can pray, "Help me, Jesus." Jesus *will* give you His help and the power of the Holy Spirit.

That doesn't mean it'll always be easy. Often life wasn't easy for Jesus either. That's why He understands how you feel. He knows about every one of your problems. And He loves you so much that He died on the cross for you. He promised to always be with you— no matter what you face.

Sometimes you may think it's hard to follow Jesus. If you need to say no to a temptation, you may wonder, "Is it worth it?" But when you *do* say no, you can look back later and think, "Whew! I'm glad I made that choice!" When you think about places where you could have fallen into the mud, you'll be able to tell yourself, "Wow! Jesus helped me escape that!"

Then, as you look ahead, you'll know that with each good choice you make, you'll be less likely to be limited in your choices when you grow up.

That's the miracle of dreaming big. That's having ideals and sticking to them. That's wanting with all your heart to follow in the footsteps of Jesus Christ.

The God of miracles created you. His promise is forever: *"I made you and will care for you; I will give you help and rescue you"* (Isaiah 46:4, GNB).

It's your life. The choices are up to you. But there's Someone always ready to help. His name is *Jesus.*

WORD LIST

abdomen (AB-doe-men) stomach

abortion (uh-BOR-shun) removal of an unborn baby from the womb before it is able to survive

acne (AK-nee) blackheads and pimples on the face and other parts of the body; often called "zits"

AIDS a disease caused by a virus (VI-rus) that destroys the body's ability to fight off illness; the letters stand for Acquired Immune Deficiency Syndrome

amniotic sac (am-nee-OT-ik sak) a bag full of liquid that protects the developing baby; also called bag of waters

anus (A-nus) opening through which solid waste passes out of the body

179

cervix (SUR-viks) opening between the uterus and the vagina

chromosome (CROW-muh-sohm) tiny thread-like particles that contain the genes received from both parents

circumcision (sur-come-SIZH-un) a minor operation that removes the loose fold of skin on a penis

clitoris (KLIT-o-ris) small, sensitive organ located just above a girl's urethra

conception (con-SEP-shun) when a sperm cell and an egg cell unite and God begins a new life

egg female sex cell; also called ovum (OH-vum)

erection (ih-REK-shun) when the penis becomes firm and stands out from the body

Fallopian tubes (fa-LOH-pee-an) passageways that receive the female sex cell on its way to the uterus

fertilization (fur-til-eye-ZAY-shun) when a sperm cell joins an egg cell

fraternal twins (fra-TUR-nal) two sperm fertilize two eggs, and two babies are born at the same time; may be the same sex, or one a girl and the other a boy

gene (jean) carries the hereditary traits that children receive from their parents

genitals (JEN-ah-tals) the external sex organs of boys or girls

homosexuality (hoh-mo-sek-shoo-AL-ah-tee) sexual relationship between two people of the same sex

hormone (HOR-mohn) starts the development of sexual traits in a boy or a girl

identical twins (i-DEN-ti-kal) a single fertilized egg grows into two babies instead of one; they will be of the same sex, born at the same time, and very similar in appearance

immune system (ih-MUNE SIS-tum) parts of the body that work together to fight against sickness

masturbation (mas-ter-BAY-shun) the handling of one's own sexual organs for pleasure

menstruation (men-stroo-AY-shun) release of tissue, egg, and waste blood from a girl's uterus, occurs about every twenty-eight days; also called a "period"

nutrient (NEW-tree-ent) the nourishment received from food

ovary (OH-va-ree) female reproductive organ that contains thousands of tiny eggs

ovulation (oh-vue-LAY-shun) time when an ovary releases an egg; usually occurs monthly

pituitary gland (pi-TOO-ah-tare-ee) master gland of the body, sends messages to other glands about growth and bodily functions

placenta (plah-CEN-tah) an organ that develops along with a growing baby during pregnancy and provides nourishment and oxygen for the baby

pornography (por-NOG-rah-fee) words and pictures that make sex dirty

181

puberty (PEW-bur-tee) the time at which a girl or boy becomes physically able to reproduce life

pubic (PEW-bik) the lowest part of the abdomen

sanitary napkin (SAN-ah-ter-ee) pad that absorbs menstrual flow and protects clothing during a girl's monthly period

scrotum (SKRO-tum) small bag of skin that holds the testicles; behind the penis

semen (SEE-men) combination of milky liquid and sperm produced by boys

sexual intercourse (SEX-shoo-al IN-ter-korse) a man's penis becomes firm and fits into a woman's vagina

sperm (spurm) male sex cell

tampon (TAM-pon) small roll of absorbent material inserted into a girl's vagina to absorb menstrual flow

testicles (TES-ti-kuls) the two male reproductive glands where sperm are produced

umbilical cord (um-BILL-i-kal) cord through which nourishment and oxygen flow from the mother to the baby during pregnancy; connected to the placenta and the baby's stomach

urethra (you-REE-thra) tube through which urine passes out of the body; in the male this tube also carries semen

uterus (YOU-ter-us) pear-shaped organ that holds a growing baby; called womb in the Bible

vagina (va-GINE-ah) birth canal through which a baby passes to be born

wet dream also called nocturnal emission (nok-TUR-nal e-MISH-un); release of excess semen during sleep

womb (woom) the word the Bible uses for uterus; the place where a baby grows until ready for birth

Answers to matching questions for "Mitzi Looks in the Mirror" on page 23.

1. d	7. c
2. b	8. f
3. g	9. a
4. h	10. k
5. i	11. j
6. e	

Answers to matching questions for "Rob and Dad Talk" on page 30.

1. i	5. a
2. f	6. d
3. e, g	7. b
4. c	8. h